Views, Positions, Legacies
Interviews with German and British Theatre Artists, 1985-2007

Edited by

Daniel Meyer-Dinkgräfe

CAMBRIDGE SCHOLARS PUBLISHING

Views, Positions, Legacies: Interviews with German and British Theatre Artists, 1985-2007, edited by Daniel Meyer-Dinkgräfe

This book first published 2007 by

Cambridge Scholars Publishing

15 Angerton Gardens, Newcastle, NE5 2JA, UK

British Library Cataloguing in Publication Data
A catalogue record for this book is available from the British Library

ISBN 1-84718-294-1; ISBN 13: 9781847182944

TABLE OF CONTENTS

ACKNOWLEDGMENTS

I am grateful to all theatre artists for giving me their time for conducting the interviews with them, and to their input in the editing of the version printed in this volume. Every effort was made to get permission for publication for the final version from all artists, but some did not respond to repeated letters and emails. I have interpreted their silence as permission.

INTRODUCTION

Part I: Plays about Famous Artists

Careful research in the manuscript and playscript sections of the British Library reveals that between 1900 and 1977, about eighty plays were written whose main character is a famous artist, compared to well over two 300 such plays in the much shorter time period of 1978—2004 (Meyer-Dinkgräfe, 2005). For the purposes of this book, a "famous artist" is a representative of any branch of the arts, i.e., not merely a fine artist, but also a musician, composer, conductor, actor, director, scenographer, etc. There is no doubt that every drama is fiction. The plays in question show, in the "dramatised reality" characters of the "historical reality", i.e. artists who have gained fame while living or posthumously.

The book collects a range of personal statements by dramatists (Pam Gems, Vanessa Drucker, Stephen MacDonald, David Pownall) , directors (Howard Davies and Roland Rees) actors (Peter Kelly, Timothy West, Margaret Wolfit, Tom Wilkinson, Miriam Margolyes) and theatre critic Irving Wardle.

A close look at the British biographical plays about famous artists reveals that the dramatists made varying use of "historical reality" in different plays. As sources for "historical reality" they used autobiographies, letters, statements of contemporaries, or biographies. The "historical reality" refers to situations in which the historical artists found themselves; it refers, moreover, to the artists' friends and family, to their sympathies and antipathies, enmities against the artist and their character traits. I propose a sliding scale that measures the degree to which dramatists make us of "historical reality" in the "dramatised reality". One pole will indicate a play that takes very much of "historical reality" into "dramatised reality". Such a play can be said to be most authentic. "Authentic" here means the orientation of the "dramatised" to the "historical" reality. A high degree of authenticity can be found in one-person-shows about historical artists which constitute a compilation of excerpts from letters, diaries, or autobiographies of the artist whose life is dramatised in that play. The opposite pole indicates plays that are least authentic: plays for which the dramatists took the life of a historical artist merely as an inspiration for a play about an artist. The artist characters in

such plays do not even carry the names of their historical sources. Tom
Kempinski's *Duet for One* (1081), about a violinist suffering from MS,
was inspired by the similar case of cellist Jacqueline du Pré (1945-1987).
In Ronald Harwood's *The Dresser*, the central artist character is Sir, an old
actor-manager. Since the author was, early on in his career, dresser to one
of the last actor-managers, Sir Donald Wolfit, Harwood might have
created the character of Sir with Wolfit in mind. Harwood was at pains to
emphasise, however, that

> Sir is not Wolfit. Norman's [the dresser of the title] relationship with Sir is
> not mine with Wolfit. Her ladyship [Sir's wife in the play] is quite unlike
> Rosalind Iden (Lady Wolfit). (1980, 9)

Apart from the level of authenticity presented in biographical plays about
famous artists, another criterion of classification is the function of the
artist characters within the plays. Edna O'Brien's *Virginia* (1981) and
Stephen MacDonald's *Not About Heroes* (1983) focus on the famous
artists' lives directly, whereas in others, the historical artist characters
serve the function to exemplify a wider issue. In Christopher Hampton's
Tales from Hollywood (1983), for example, Bertolt Brecht and Thomas
and Heinrich Mann represent, among others, those artists who emigrated
from Germany to Hollywood during the Second World War. Brecht tries
hard to use his time in Hollywood as much as possible to change the world
through theatre. Thomas Mann is able to perceive the suffering of those
remaining behind in Germany and tries to help, albeit ineffectually in his
elitist-intellectual ways. The character of Heinrich Mann serves to
emphasise the general feeling of loneliness of all the emigrants in a
foreign country. Together, the artist characters exemplify the issues of
political inefficiency and cowardice of the emigrant artists and
intellectuals: "The intellectual is inefficient, politics and society
overpower him, which is to a large degree his own fault" (Westecker
1983).

Dusty Hughes' *Futurists* (1986) shows the artistic-intellectual life of
Russia in 1921, only a few years after the revolution. Among the play's
characters are Mayakovsky, Anna Akhmatova, Osip Mandelstam,
Alexander Blok, Kolia Gumilyov, Lili Brik and Maxim Gorki. Those artist
characters mirror the unrest of their time. Different groupings of the artists
try to develop the form of art most suitable to express the revolution, with
its fundamental changes of inner and outer life.

Master Class by David Pownall (1983) represents middle ground
between biographical plays about famous artists that focus on the artists
for the artist's sake and those in which the artist characters serve a more

general function. The artist characters in *Master Class*, Prokofiev and Shostakovich, demonstrate that art cannot be prescribed and purpose-made to serve an ultimately un-artistic goal. In that sense, art and artists are independent, in this case of dictator Stalin's moods: the play is set in 1948, in a Kremlin antechamber. Stalin has summoned the two composers to explain to them personally (assisted by culture secretary Andrej Zhdanov) what correct and good Soviet music should be like. Apart from focusing on the political implications of the (fictional) encounter of the four main characters, Pownall manages to present the composers' suffering and their abilities of maintaining their personal dignities and artistic integrities under duress.

A third criterion for differentiating among biographical plays about famous artists is the constellation of characters within the plays. Some plays show artists mainly among themselves, such as Mozart and Salieri in Shaffer's *Amadeus*, Prokofiev and Shostakovich in Pownall's *Master Class*, poets Owen and Sassoon in MacDonald's *Not About Heroes* and Alice B. Toklas and Gertrude Stein in Wells's *Gertrude Stein and a Companion*. Other plays present a wider picture, placing a central artist character amongst several other characters, not necessarily including other artists.

Where do those biographical plays fit in with contemporary British drama as a whole? The beginning of a new era in the development of 20th century British drama is usually identified with the first performance of John Osborne's *Look Back in Anger* on the 8th of May 1956. The original assumption that this play constitutes a revolution of British theatre had, later on, to be revised in favour of the insight that *Look Back in Anger* is a development of previously existing traditions regarding both form and content. Osborne and other dramatists of his time expressed the feelings of that generation: they were disappointed about post-war developments. On the personal level, many had benefitted from the law on education of 1944, which was introduced to enable working-class children easier access to school and university (Dietrich 1974, 745). Although improved possibilities of education are desirable, in this case they led to a state of disorientation and to the children's alienation from their original social environment, which was not necessarily replaced by new social connections. The resultant disillusionment of the young generation on the personal level was enhanced by political events such as the Suez-crisis, the Russian invasion of Hungary and the beginning of the Cold War. Many of the dramatists belonged to the working class themselves (Osborne, Wesker, Pinter). In dramatizing the problems of their own generation, they frequently wrote about social groups that had hardly been characters in drama before: the working classes, adolescents, old and ill people. The way of presentation was often naturalistic (Tynan 1984, 178). John Russell Taylor has thoroughly analysed this phase and the title of his book has coined its name: *Anger and After* (1962).

The social and political events of 1968, the student unrests, the crushing of the democratisation in Prague, the Vietnam War and the Cultural revolution in China were indirectly reflected in the British theatre scene. One indication is the significant increase of alternative theatres: Wolter lists sixteen new establishments in 1968, such as Portable Theatre, Interaction, Pip Simmons Group and Red Ladder Theatre (1980, 136). These so-called "fringe theatres" formed a forum for the young and politically oriented dramatists. They wanted to

> integrate theatre more strongly into day-to-day life. The general tendency
> was to make the spectator not look up to an elevated sphere of culture, but
> to bring theatre literally to the people: onto the street, into the factory, into
> the pub, into youth hostels and local communication centres. (Enkemann
> 1980, 499)

Another very important factor in this time was the abolition of censorship, which enabled more and different subject-matters to be treated on the British stage than before. Many dramatists who wrote at that time were socialist, such as David Hare, Howard Brenton, Trevor Griffiths and Stephen Poliakoff. But dramatists such as Stoppard, Gray, Hampton, Ayckbourn, Bond, Shaffer, Storey and Pinter also pursued traditional genres further (Hayman 1979, 68-70).

Approximately around the middle of the seventies the original verve, which had arisen at the end of the sixties, decreased considerably. Dramatists' concern shifted from general political and theoretical questions to a more individual perspective. This tendency continued throughout the eighties, with an emphasis on the following subject-matters: questions of education (e.g. Willy Russell, *Educating Rita* [1986]; Simon Gray, *Quartermaion's Terms* [1983]); the situation of disabled people (e.g. Brian Clark, *Whose Life is it Anyway* [1978]; Phil Young, *Crystal Clear* [1983]); the role of man and woman and the importance of the family (e.g. Caryl Churchill, *Top Girls* [1982]); the conflict in Northern Ireland (e.g. *Translations* [1980] and other plays by Brian Friel); the nuclear threat (e.g. Brian Clark, *The Petition* [1986]); national socialism (e.g. C.P.Taylor, *Good* [1981]), as well as plays about the concerns of the English middle classes (e.g. Alan Ayckbourn, *Season's Greetings* [1982]). Problems of the individual are central to all those plays. This statement holds true especially for the plays that are at the centre of Part I of this book: plays about famous historical artists.

Part II: Boulevard Comedy in Germany

Twenty major German cities have a total of twenty-four theatres specializing, at a high level of sophistication, in presenting light comedy. Theatre artists, journalists, academics and critics refer to them as *boulevard comedy theatres* that present productions of *boulevard comedy*. According to official annual statistics of sold seats, in almost all cases, boulevard comedy theatres have been able to attract larger audiences than municipal or state theatres in the same cities. Such commercial success is remarkable in a fiercely competitive market. Boulevard comedy theatres are predominantly privately run, with only two exceptions that receive public subsidy. They have their own typical ambience and principles of artistic management and casting. There are playwrights, actors, directors and designers who work almost exclusively in boulevard comedy, developing highly specialised approaches to their work. This part of the book collects a range of interviews with artistic directors of these theatres, some of whom also serve as actors in their own theatres, and one dramaturg. The plays are light comedy, sometimes with darker undertones, often placing their ordinary middle class characters within extraordinary situations, much in the tradition of farce.

Geographically, twenty-three of the twenty-four boulevard comedy theatres in Germany are spread evenly across the former West Germany: Berlin, Bochum, Bonn, Braunschweig, Cologne, Darmstadt, Düsseldorf, Duisburg, Frankfurt, Fürth, Hamburg, Hannover, Heilbronn, Karlsruhe, Kassel, Münster, Munich, Stuttgart and Wuppertal. Dresden is so far the only city of the former East Germany to possess a boulevard comedy theatre. Seventeen boulevard comedy theatres have the word *comedy* in their name, spelt either conventionally Komödie, or more progressively, Comödie. Some theatres refer to their location in their name, either the city (e.g., Komödie Düsseldorf[1]), or an area or within the city: for example, Düsseldorf's second boulevard comedy theatre is located near the main shopping street of the town, Königsallee, or Kö for short and calls itself Theater an der Kö. The boulevard comedy theatre in Cologne is located close to the famous cathedral and thus calls itself Theater am Dom. The only boulevard comedy theatre to be located within a five-star hotel is Munich's Komödie im Bayerischen Hof. One of the three boulevard comedy theatres in Wuppertal is called m&m theatre, taking the first letters of the founder and artistic directors' last names: Misiorny and Mueller. Another boulevard comedy theatre named after its founder is the Waldau Theater Komödie Bremen, which started as a theatre dedicated to presenting plays in the regional dialect of Bremen and added boulevard comedy to the repertory and the word Komödie to its name only in 2002.[2]

At the head of each boulevard comedy theatres in Germany is the *Intendant*, who combines artistic and managerial - administrative functions. The restricted budget of boulevard comedy theatres does not often allow a split of artistic and managerial functions, such as is more and more frequent at larger German municipal or state theatres. Across the country, the older artistic managers, who founded the major boulevard comedy theatres in the 1950s and 1960s, are gradually retiring and making way for a new generation with fresh ideas and initiatives for their theatres. The majority of boulevard comedy theatres have to survive without subsidies of any kind, though some receive a minor subsidy. One of the boulevard comedy theatres that is most heavily subsidised, the Komödie im Marquardt in Stuttgart, still relies on box office receipts for forty per cent of its annual budget. The Komödienhaus in Heilbronn is the exception in the boulevard comedy theatre scene in Germany, in that it is a newly built venue of that town's fully subsidised municipal theatre.

The twenty-four boulevard comedy theatres in Germany together produce more than 100 plays per year. They are a considerable factor in Germany's theatre scene. Yet academic consideration of boulevard comedy theatre in Germany has been very limited. In his 1968 history of comedy, Prang explicitly excludes the discussion of boulevard comedy because such plays do not really want to do more than entertain their audiences for one night in the theatre (1968: 364). Similarly, Schoell, writing particularly about post-second-world-war French drama, states that the sole intention of boulevard theatre is to entertain its audiences. The spectators are those who want to spend a good amount of money to purchase pleasant entertainment without much strain and if the boulevard theatres do not offer such entertainment any more, such spectators are likely to go to a striptease club instead (Schoell, 1970: 69). The plays in the boulevard theatres, Schoell argues further, have been the same since they first appeared: they did not undergo any genuine development of either language or form. Haida disagrees: a development has taken place when boulevard comedies deny their spectators the happy ending, characteristic of conventional plays in the boulevard comedy canon (1973: 157). Weckherlin summarises that in Germany, boulevard comedy theatre carries the stigma of the trivial, with its synonyms of banality, shallowness, flatness, meaninglessness and insignificance (2001: 21). Leisentritt's 1979 Ph.D. thesis, *Das Eindimensionale Theater*, shares this general approach. Weckherlin's 1992 MA thesis discusses the production of Ayckbourn's *Henceforward* at one of the two Berlin boulevard comedy theatres directed by the renowned Peter Zadek (b. 1926), focusing on the four ways in which this production broke the norms of theatre in general and boulevard comedy theatre in particular: first, the fact that Zadek, the artistic manager of the largest state theatre (Deutsches Schauspielhaus Hamburg) directed at a privately run boulevard comedy theatre; second, what Zadek made of the production itself; third, that actors usually appearing at the state theatres now made their debuts at boulevard comedy theatres; and finally, the impact such a production has on the audience of a boulevard comedy theatre.

Part III: Academia, Theory and Practice

Two British theatre artists feature in the interviews in Part III: David Ian Rabey combines his job as a professor of Drama and Theatre at the University of Wales Aberystwyth with an active career as a theatre actor, director and dramatist. Mike Pearson is a performance practitioner and professor of Performance Studies in the same university department.

Part IV Legacies

The final part of the book provides a range of interviews both from the UK and from Germany, starting off with Sir Richard Eyre's account of his seminal production of *Hamlet* at the Royal Court in 1980. German Director Heinz-Uwe Haus combines the legacy of Brecht (he trained with some of Brecht's foremost disciples) and politics (Haus lived and worked in the former German Democratic Republic—the totalitarian regime's repression influenced his everyday life and work considerably). Ursula Dinkgräfe, finally, represents both personal legacy and the numerous well-trained and highly capable and successful actors across the world who do not (want to) attain star-status.

PART I:

PLAYS ABOUT FAMOUS ARTISTS

CHAPTER ONE

THE ROYAL SHAKESPEARE COMPANY AND *PIAF:* PAM GEMS

Pam Gems[1] wrote the play *Piaf*[2] about Edith Piaf[3]. Letter to DMD in May, 1985

DMD
During the last few years, the number of plays about poets, composers, actors, etc. (in short, artists) has increased considerably. Could you think of an explanation for this remarkable development?

PG
A move away from the Brechtian, perhaps... something to do with the move to the right.

DMD
Among those plays, a large number are "one-person-shows" or two-handers. Do you think this is only because of financial/commercial reasons?

PG
Yes.

DMD
What is the function of a "bio-play"? Does it intend to give an insight into the life of a famous artist, or to convey a more universal message?

PG
The second.

DMD

Please comment on the relation of fact and fiction in your play.

PG

Plays deal not with facts, but with truth. The use of any theme, life of a person is a metaphor. There is a value, to the dramatist. By beginning with someone known, you have a coagulation of ideas, impressions, views, ready to hand. These you develop or overturn. By creating new characters in a play, you must spend time acquainting the audience with these characters, this is why dramatists have often used known characters. It is a form of shorthand.

DMD

In your opinion, what part does suffering play in the artist's life? Is it a prerequisite to good quality in the artist's creation?

PG

Does God exist?

DMD

What do you think is the artist's relation to love, sex (emotions in general)?

PG

Same as anybody else's

DMD

Do you think that "bio-plays" about artists are an attempt of the dramatist to come to terms with being an artist him/herself by experiencing what it was for someone else to have been an artist?

PG

No.

DMD

What inspired you to write the play?

PG

I was asked to write a vehicle for a Rumanian actress who was finding it difficult to get work in England.

DMD
What sources did you use?

PG
Three biographies, many newspaper and magazine cuttings, a great many conversations with people who knew or had worked with Piaf. Which I then threw away.

DMD
Which characteristics of Piaf did you want to present most?

PG
I was not writing a documentary, therefore I was not interested in a facsimile portrait. Piaf's work speaks for her.

DMD
Please describe any cooperation with the director and the actors of the play's production.

PG
I saw very little of director or cast.

DMD
Please comment on the response by theatre critics.

PG
I am not interested in value judgments from critics, only in whether their notices are selling notices or not ... in other words, in what manner they are attempting to affect my livelihood. I was interested in two themes .. the effect on a human being of "fame" .. exposure, what it does to the soul. And I was interested in trying to convey the true feeling of the performer's life .. the stresses, discomforts .. the actuality, as an antidote to the usual "backstage" notions of performance life depicted by such plays as for example *Noises Off*[4], or many Hollywood movies. I was also interested in the notion of a human being who did not change her class or modify her stringent view of life when the "good life" came her way.

Notes

1. Born in 1925, Pam Gems began writing plays only after her children had grown up. In the 60s and 70s, she had been interested in the feminist movement, and in socialist politics. Feminism in its broadest sense is at the centre of her plays, such

as *Queen Christina* (Royal Shakespeare Company, 1977), *Piaf* (Royal Shakespeare Company, 1978, directed by Howard Davies, with Jane Lapotaire as Piaf), or *Camille* (Royal Shakespeare Company, 1982). Some critics consider such adaptations of existing material, or versions of Chekhov's *Uncle Vanya*, 1992) and *The Blue Angel* (1992) as more successful than original plays such as *Deborah's Daughter* (1994). At the Royal National Theatre, John Caird directed *Stanley* (1996), with Anthony Sher in the title role of painter Stanley Spencer. In 1997, Gems added *Marlene*, a play about Marlene Dietrich to her canon of bio-plays. (Meyer-Dinkgräfe 2002, 99-100)

2 Gems, Pam. 1979. *Piaf*, Oxford: Amber Lane.

3 Edith Piaf (1915-1963) was a famous French singer.

4 *Noises Off* was written by Michael Frayn (b. 1933). It deals with life in the theatre from the backstage perspective and has been commercially successful on stage since 1982. In 1992 a film version followed.

CHAPTER TWO

DIRECTING *PIAF:*
HOWARD DAVIES

Howard Davies[1], director of the first production of *Piaf* by Pam Gems.
Interview with DMD on 29.3.1985

DMD
Among plays about artists, there is a large number of one-person shows.
Could you think of any artistic reasons for this development?

HD
I can find no artistic merit in one-man shows. Sorry, but I find them dull.
It seems to me they are like novels, like biographies. I do not think of them
as theatre. I could listen to them on tape, or on the radio. The fact of
having an actor give vocal expression to a line is less interesting than to
have him on stage.

DMD
What is the function of a biographical play about an artist? Does it intend
to give an insight into the life of the artist, or to convey a more universal
message?

HD
Piaf is the one I directed. I think it had a message beyond the artist's life.
Pam Gems came to theatre writing late because she had deliberately made
a choice, which was to bring up her children: she did not commit herself to
writing till they were well into their teens. At a particular time when Pam
had actually been through family, had brought them up, she was going to
meetings that were among the strong feminist groupings in the early
seventies in this country. She looked for a way of expressing two things,
one of which was drama, and also to take for a central figure, which is rare
in the theatre, a woman. In the case of Piaf it was somebody whom she

remembered, it was her generation. She took a character that was essentially working class and in the course of an extraordinary sort of career she managed neither to loose her class and her allegiance to her class nor her allegiance to that particular brand of feminism which was—which is—innate in that kind of character, or in those kinds of people. That is, she saw women as being initiators in love, who are certainly not dependent upon men. And so in a highly inarticulate way, rather than in an articulate middle-class feminism that Pam did not particularly want to write about, because it then would be a piece of polemics, she saw the character to be the best way to express her particular politics. Therefore the play was less about the songs than it was about how that woman managed—in a male world—to survive and hang on to take the mike and sing.

DMD
Could you please comment on any kind of cooperation with Pam Gems during rehearsals?

HD
She was not present in rehearsals, partly because we were rehearsing in Stratford and she does not like travelling very much. In the previous nine months Pam and I had worked endlessly on the script. When I first read the script it was fairly long, some scenes slightly recurrent. It included several characters who I found were duplications, and it needed to be trimmed, cut and edited. For example, in the case of the songs you can take all the famous songs; it was distressing for Pam to hear it from me, and she did not want to let go for some time, but I had to say that—I won the argument—that for any actress it would be tough to stand up and sing the famous songs of Piaf: the audience knew the songs and some of them had actually seen Piaf sing them herself. They would say: 'well, this is not like my memory'. The play was not meant to be a trip down memory lane. It was much better if an actress had a chance to sing, let's say, the least well-known songs, whereby the audience would listen to the words and not recall their memories and make a judgment. Thus I said it was much better to dispense with the famous songs, and maybe only fit in, at the very end, when she dies on stage, "Je ne regrette rien", that alone. In other words: deal with the off-beat, because the play essentially was off-beat, and it would allow the lyrics of the songs to come through, which we were going to do in English. That was another debate. It took us a very long time talking about whether we should translate the songs and sing them in English as we would do them in Cockney. I approached one actress to play

the part at the same time as I was approaching Jane Lapotaire[3], who said: "I see it essentially as a Parisienne voice, I have to have a French accent", which I thought completely bananas because what Pam had written was a cockney sparrow, which is an English idiomatic equivalent to what the character stood for in France. Therefore when we approached the songs, we thought, well, should we rather translate, and how can this cockney sparrow get up and sing in French? But then the play broke all the rules anyway, with regard to its staging or its location. There were all sorts of debates like that because she had thrown the play up into the air, and I tried to sort out whether there was a way of putting it on stage that had consistency. It would be much shorter than what she had written. For example, Josephine Baker was in it the first time; you got Marlene Dietrich and Josephine Baker. You do not need the two of them. You need one character who is a counterpoint to Piaf at a point at which she is at the height of her success, and probably what you need is this aristocrat, this very, very beautiful woman, this very aristocratic success.

DMD
How did you prepare for directing the play?

HD
I read the sister's biography; most of the cast read that as well. We also dug out as much film footage as we could and we had translations of her newspaper reviews on her shows, also those of her shows in America. So quite a lot of research was done, on the auto-biographical account of her life. In a way it became less important as we went into rehearsals. That was good to have at the back of our head, but it was not the play.

DMD
What made you choose Jane Lapotaire as Piaf?

HD
There were certain actresses that I had admired. I talked to Trevor Nunn[4] about it and put my short list of about five to him. And he voted for somebody else. I had never met Jane before, so I met her. She did a small audition for me, she was already quite successful at the time, she had been in a very successful TV version on Marie Curie in which she had made some kind of a household name. I got on with her, we got on with each other and at the very end of the audition I said: "And do you sing?" And she said yes. I did not bother to find out, and it was not before two months later that she told me that she could not sing. Well, it was too late now,

and she got away with it. And she got into a terrible panic about it. I mean she really could not sing. She had to learn to sing. I had already heard that she, when she had gone for a part in a TV film they said: "Do you ride a motorbike?" she said: "Yes, I've been riding motorbikes for the last eight years." They started filming in a week's time and she had to learn it in a week. I mean she got the job because she is that sort of woman, she'd just do anything.

DMD
What was the main emphasis in your direction?

HD
With hindsight it is easier to see that probably what one looked for in the character was never known to the introspection, but introspection is something that is acquired through education or class or leisure time. Her quality was to be always on the move. Her way of coping with moments of deep depression, or addiction, or indeed anything you read in the biographies was by going forward, was by actually attacking, so that any tendency of the script to allow her to soliloquise, to be meditative, introspective at all, was pushed forward. In other words, she became quite raucous, vulgar and aggressive so that the emotionality of the part became greater in the course of the evening because one could see that she was overcompensating for moments when she was about to trip over, moments when she got inadequate. She would shout, scream at people, abuse them, cry to gain attention, all completely unexpected. But it was not necessarily a conscious decision when we went into rehearsal. It was not difficult to discuss that from the script, because Pam had written a series of vignettes. She had not written a sequential, narrative script. She had said: 'I'll take a little of this and a little of that. And this arrangement of scenes will actually give you the finished picture'. There is thus no synthesis which we call Edith Piaf. The moments in her life are grabbed by this very hungry animal. Again with hindsight one might say this added up to a life of extraordinary bravura. If we had tried to change location all the time in conjunction with the script—in a lift, in an aeroplane, in a bedroom, in New York, in a nightclub—it would drive you completely balmy. We just had an empty stage and six chairs and allowed the characters to speak. That way everything is very fast. The audience are allowed to place, in their minds, one scene against the other, in counterpoints. Otherwise, the counterpoint is blocked. We had a problem of style, as well. The first part of each scene, let us say the first five or six lines, would be exposition, and anybody could speak these lines, they were not character lines. And then

you got a piece of quite real dialogue, quite tough dialogue, fairly abrasive, usually quite witty, and then there would be a gag, a joke, finishing up the scene. We did not know how to make these scenes work, I mean in what style we should make the scenes. Should it be high burlesque, for example? In the second week in rehearsals I asked the cast to tell jokes. Most English jokes are built like small plays: 'a man goes into a bar with a polar bear and says to the barman...' There would be a piece of dialogue and then there is a punch line. Eventually we worked on jokes, dramatizing jokes, for about a week, doing it very quickly; someone would tell a joke and people would get up and dramatize it. The level of invention among the cast was very good. We got very, very professional at that, being able to set up the scene very quickly through dialogue; not by saying, you understand, this is what is happening, not by talking to the audience, but by doing it. Then we went back to Pam's script and that was the style we should do it in. You come on to the stage very fast, you establish who the characters are, in the lines that are given and then you can play the scene, however long it is, two pages, one page, half a page. And then, usually, there was a rather rude line, an abrasive line. If you work at the Royal Shakespeare Company you work on the text a lot. At least at the time I was working on a lot of writers and their scripts trying to work out how the script developed. I became aware that that is how Pam Gems wrote. She was not interested in a kind of naturalistic, social, realistic way of setting up a recognizable scene. She was only interested in saying: this is all you needed to know in order to be able to understand the following conversation.

DMD
Could you comment on the relationship between fact and fiction in *Piaf*, please?

HD
I do not think much of it was fiction except for example she never met Marlene Dietrich; scenes like that are a dramatic way of expressing an idea that she is one person who has dedicated her life, cynically dedicated her life to glamour. Piaf actually said: I ignore it. When we did the play in New York, on Broadway, there was a lot of protest from the Edith Piaf fan clubs who said this is a travesty of her life; they were outraged, so I assume they were romanticizing the figure.

DMD
What was the critical response like?

HD

It was flattering because in England we had very good reviews. It was different when we went to America, because in the States they said: 'This is unlikely'. They did actually criticize it on the level that it was too rude, too crude, too loosely put together and that it did not add up to a portrait of fame and fortune. That has to do with an American belief that if somebody becomes notorious or famous then therefore they have within them the germ of genius. They do not see that as being necessarily an arduous struggle by somebody who is as obdurate as Piaf was towards fate, or a circumstance. They do not see it in that way, politically. They see that the best people will rise to the surface. And therefore, politically, their view of the play was less warm than in this country.

DMD

Do you think that suffering is a prerequisite to good quality in the artist's creation?

HD

That is nonsense. I do not think that was contained in Pam's play What I find unpalatable about such an idea is that dramatists, if they are going to write that or discern that, assume a rift between the public persona and the private person—a schematising and hackneyed theme. They see it the wrong way round. That is a romantic way of looking at it, you know, self-mutilation to ennoble the soul...

DMD

Do you think that "bio-plays" about artists are an attempt of the dramatist to come to terms with being an artist him/herself by experiencing what it was for someone else to have been an artist?

HD

Certainly under the Thatcher government as the present one, there always has been a certain amount of guilt about being an artist. Take someone like Edward Bond[5]: his *Saved* caused outrage in this country. There is no doubt that that particular play and the storm that grew all around it publicly and in the critical circle, gave rise to the abolition of censorship in this country. But it has also a very serious effect on Bond as a playwright—I'm not sure whether Edward Bond would refute what I am saying. He was writing with an extremely good ear for urban working-class language, and also particularly a sharp eye for the dehumanising effects of post-war society in which he grew up. He was writing contemporary plays about contemporary issues. What happened at that time was that journalists who masquerade as critics, said: 'You leave contemporary politics to us, we are journalists, you are artists'. And from that time on, Edward Bond wrote parable plays, set historically. I think amongst most playwrights, and certainly most playwrights in the RSC would acknowledge without question the fact that it is far easier to get good reviews for plays that are set historically, or about artists, because it makes it safe. It is easy to have that as an after-dinner conversation where it becomes maybe heated, but it is always safe. If you talk about whether *Saved* is truthful or not, you then have this problem about whether it is truthful or factual, because it is about contemporary England. Yes, there is a certain push in the direction that artists should deal with artists, should deal with history, with artistic subjects, from the journalists and the people who actually provide grants in what is essentially a state-subsidized theatre set-up in this country. But as a result there also is this feeling of guilt. We should be dealing with contemporary issues and our own obsession with relevant artists in their own time is probably an understandable action.

Notes

1 Howard Davies (b. 1945) began his career in the theatre in 1968 as assistant stage manager at the Birmingham Repertory Company. From 1972-4 he was associate director at Bristol Old Vic, since 1976 he has been associated with the Royal Shakespeare Company, where he directed Edward Bond's *Bingo* (1976), *Piaf* by Pam Gems (1978, with Jane Lapotaire), and Christopher Hampton's adaptation of *Les Liaisons Dangereuses* (1985, with Alan Rickman and Juliet Stevenson). Since 1988, Davies has also been associated with the National Theatre, where his productions include Ibsen's *Hedda Gabler* with Juliet Stevenson (1989), David Hare's *The Secret Rapture* (1989), Arthur Miller's *The Crucible* (1990) and Schiller's *Maria Stuart* (1996). More recent work includes a revival of Albee's *Who's Afraid of Virginia Woolf?* at the Almeida with Diana Rigg, Richard Nelson's *The General from America* (1997), and *Wassa* after Gorky (1999), both at the Royal National Theatre. Throughout his career, Davies has placed much emphasis on structural and conceptual clarity, allowing his actors to go beyond intellectual understanding in developing deeply felt emotions. (Meyer-Dinkgräfe 2002, 64-5)
2 Gems, Pam. 1979. *Piaf*, Oxford: Amber Lane.
3 Jane Lapotaire (b. 1944) played the part of Piaf in Howard Davies' production.
4 Trevor Nunn (b.1940)was artistic director at the Royal Shakespeare Company between 1968—78. In 1997 he succeeded Richard Eyre as director of the Royal National Theatre, choosing Christopher Hampton's version of Ibsen's *An Enemy of the People* as first his production, starring Ian McKellen, set design by John Napier, followed by a revival of Pinter's *Betrayal*, *Mutabilitie* by Frank McGuinness, and the musical *Oklahoma!*. (Meyer-Dinkgräfe 2002, 222)

5 Edward Bond (b. 1934) achieved notoriety in the theatre with his play *Saved* (Royal Court, 1965), especially the scene in which a group of adolescents stone a baby to death in its pram. Bond then turned away from drastic portrayals of contemporary life, writing rather about the past as a mirror of the present, as in *Early Morning* (1968) and *Lear* (1971), a version of Shakespeare's *King Lear*. Revivals of his plays are produced worldwide. (Meyer-Dinkgräfe 2002, 35).

CHAPTER THREE

AN AMERICAN *PIAF*:
VANESSA DRUCKER

Vanessa Drucker[1], author of *No Regrets*[2] about Piaf, in a letter to DMD, 31. 8. 1985

DMD
During the last few years, the number of plays about poets, composers, actors, etc. (in short, artists) has increased considerably. Could you think of an explanation for this remarkable development

VD
During the past few years there has been a lot of interest in "nostalgia" fads, such as art deco, Hollywood musicals of the 30's and 40's, World War stories, etc. As each decade of our modern history becomes slightly more remote, we re-examine it. Perhaps there is a connection here with an increase in biographical and historical plays.

DMD
Among those plays, a large number are "one-person-shows" or two-handers. Do you think this is only because of financial/commercial reasons?

VD
To be truthful, I do think the one and two handers are written and produced for reasons of economy.

DMD
What is the function of a "bio-play"? Does it intend to give an insight into the life of a famous artist, or to convey a more universal message?

VD

If a bioplay gives insight into an artist's work and life, it has certainly succeeded, and if it gets over an even wider message, it is an even better play.

DMD

In your opinion, what part does suffering play in the artist's life? Is it a prerequisite to good quality in the artist's creation?

VD

A certain amount of suffering produces insights, wisdom, maturity, growth, forces us to adapt and become more aware. As such I suppose an artist often uses suffering. However, I do not see an inevitable link between art and suffering, and remember much great art is produced through a sense of peace or happiness, as I imagine Mozart to have composed or Monet to have painted.

DMD

What do you think is the artist's relation to love, sex (emotions in general)?

VD

I think most artists have a strong sexuality, even if not physically expressed; art and sex are both creative activities involving imagination and ego.

DMD

Do you think that "bio-plays" about artists are an attempt of the dramatist to come to terms with being an artist him/herself by experiencing what it was for someone else to have been an artist?

VD

In my own case yes. Both in *No Regrets* and in other biographical plays I have identified with the characters I was describing.

DMD

What inspired you to write the play?

VD

I wrote the play in 1975. It was commissioned by Peter Fetterman of Fetter productions, with the intention of a presentation at the Criterion Theatre in the West End. He later decided not to pursue the option he bought on my play. Although Fetterman had been told of my interest in Piaf, the actual idea of writing on her was his and not mine.

DMD
What sources did you use?

VD
I used the biography by her sister and various newspaper clips.

DMD
Please describe any cooperation with the director and the actors of the play's production.

VD
I helped Jacke Skarvallis, who sang the role, with the French pronunciation of the songs. I had no other artistic input into the production.

DMD
Please comment on the response by theatre critics.

VD
The review by the *Stage* critic described my play as more sensitive than the Gems version, with which I agree as I do not like the Gems play. I think it overemphasizes the sensational and sordid sides of Piaf's life, not that they are not important, but I think the balance is wrong. I do not remember what the other reviews of my play said. They were moderately favourable.

Notes

1 Vanessa Drucker has worked as a freelance corporate communications writer since 1988 and has written for numerous major corporations and magazines. She specializes in the financial industries and in business development. Her assignments include writing, editing and research for brochures, newsletters, speeches, magazine articles, websites, corporate identity and naming and business plans. She is also a former Wall Street attorney, and has had wide-ranging experience in Europe. She works fluently in French, German and Italian. Before directing her focus to corporate communications, Vanessa Drucker worked as a corporate attorney at Cadwalader, Wickersham & Taft, where she was involved in asset backed financing deals, securities and banking law. She holds an MA and a BA from Cambridge University, England and is admitted to the New York Bar.

She has a Certificate in Financial Management from NYU. Vanessa Drucker contributes articles to numerous financial and business publications. Her work has appeared in: *Financial Times Online, Crain's NY Business, Barron's, Financial Executive, Global Custodian, Mergers & Acquisitions, Financial History, On Investing* (Schwab), *Business Advisor* (Wells Fargo), *Global Finance, Global* (Deloitte & Touche) and *Advisor's Resource* (Skandia). She also writes fiction about the contemporary business world: *The Big Picture*, Crown Publishers, Inc. and *Winner Takes All*, Crown Publishers, Inc. Her books have been translated into Japanese, Chinese and Italian.

2 Drucker, Vanessa. *No Regrets*. Playscript 1413

Chapter Four

Writing About Friendship: Stephen MacDonald and *Not About Heroes*

Stephen MacDonald[1], is the author of *Not About Heroes*[2], a play about Siegfried Sassoon[3] and Wilfred Owen[4]. MacDonald played the part of Sassoon on several occasions, e.g. the National Theatre production in 1986. Letter to DMD, 27.3.1985

DMD
During the last few years, the number of plays about poets, composers, actors, etc. (in short, artists) has increased considerably. Could you think of an explanation for this remarkable development

SMD
The biographical play has a long an honourable history from Aeschylus though Marlowe and Shakespeare to Shaw. The Mystery Plays were an attempt at telling the life-story of Christ. Lacking Kings, Generals and Politicians of heroic stature, I think we have turned inwards to our own heroes—the creative artists. But it's a big subject.

DMD
Among those plays, a large number are "one-person-shows" or two-handers. Do you think this is only because of financial/commercial reasons?

SMD
Yes—largely economic reasons explain the one and two character plays. It also makes it much easier to transfer the play to other theatres in other places. There is also the benefit of gaining more single-minded concentration on the subject—although too often it appears to isolate the character from his society. I took some trouble to include outside opinion in *Not About Heroes*—from Robert Graves to Winston Churchill—and

was frequently tempted to bring on some of the people who were mentioned. My new play, which has its origins in fact, has the luxury of five characters. If it works out well when I've finished it, it means that I could not possibly get on a production of it myself. (Fortunately, a London management has been interested enough to commission it from me and that gave me more freedom as far as the number of characters was concerned).

DMD
What is the function of a "bio-play"? Does it intend to give an insight into the life of a famous artist, or to convey a more universal message?

SMD
I doubt if the biographical play has a "function". I wrote *NAH* in an attempt to understand how one man (Owen) could be so deeply affected by his meeting and friendship with another (Sassoon) that his life and his poetry was transformed by it.

DMD
Please comment on the relation of fact and fiction in your play.

SMD
I prefer to stick to fact if I am using real names and places. Otherwise I can't justify offering imagination as historical truth. When there is a central mystery, as in *NAH*, my attempts to understand it seem to me to be of no value if I have not kept to the truth—even though it is only my possibly limited understanding of the truth. When there is more mystery than fact available to me, I may use real incidents but, as in my new play, I make clear the amount of fiction involved by using fictional names.

DMD
In your opinion, what part does suffering play in the artist's life? Is it a prerequisite to good quality in the artist's creation?

SMD
Suffering sharpens the sensitivity to others. Pain, physical or mental, can be a motive for creating an alternative world where the suffering is under one's control. A retreat into fantasy, perhaps. Or an imaginative effort to understand how it has come about. It's a huge subject—my own feelings about it change regularly with changing circumstances.

DMD
What do you think is the artist's relation to love, sex (emotions in general)?

SMD
The question is much too vague, I'm afraid. An artist remains a human being, or he has no right to be an artist. His emotional and sexual life is as wide and possibly as varied as anyone else's—even though more of it may be lived in his imagination.

DMD
Do you think that "bio-plays" about artists are an attempt of the dramatist to come to terms with being an artist him/herself by experiencing what it was for someone else to have been an artist?

SMD
Yes. It may not be a conscious decision to try to understand one's self, but by expressing what one knows and feels through the medium of an art form, one hopes for enough objectivity through which greater understanding may be achieved. If understanding is achieved, of course, it may well be the end of the drive to express one's self.

DMD
What inspired you to write the play?

SMD
Many things prompted me to write NAH—see above. Both of the characters had been flawed heroes of mine for a long time, and I wanted others to love and admire them as much as I did... Others outside Academic circles, that is, where an emotional understanding has frequently been assumed, if not always truly felt.

DMD
What sources did you use?

SMD
My principal sources are listed in the Faber edition of the play. Sassoon's diaries were not published when I wrote it and if I were doing the play now I would make great use of them. However, they have not in any way altered my feeling about him or his world, and the diaries do not contradict anything that the play says. But it would have made the gathering of

information much easier. I have talked to a few people who knew Sassoon as an old man and the general feeling of a soul lost in a world he no longer understood reinforced my decision to shape the play as a man with all the guilt of the survivor trying to live with the memory of what has been lost (Not, as one critic suggested, to make him old enough for me to play the part myself...)

DMD
Which characteristics of Sassoon and Owen did you want to present most?

SMD
Sassoon: Generosity, a loving nature represented by his background as well as by war experience and that same repression probably preventing him from reaching the very front rank of poets. A deeply attractive (to me) sense of humour and a wonderful sense of the ridiculous. Owen: a surface of timidity and shyness (exaggerated by shell-shock) masking a much darker area of ambition and hunger for approval and acceptance, especially sexually, which I believe is where the poems that suggest genius originate. His hero worship is very pronounced—when his love for Keats is transferred to Sassoon, he may well be reaching the stage where he can now dare to love someone living in the hope of his love being requited. Although I still find it difficult to believe that they had a sexual affair. At least a hundred other characteristics—I hope they are in the play.

DMD
Please describe any cooperation with the director and the actors of the play's production.

SMD
As I am both an actor and a director as well as a playwright I was possibly more conscious of writing thinks that actors and directors could profitably use. In the course of writing my director (Eric Standidge[5]) was closely involved and did indeed contribute some ideas, just as I was able to suggest, with his understanding and agreement, degrees of emphasis and interpretation which are part of a director's job.

DMD
Please comment on the response by theatre critics.

SMD

The critical reception of the play was warmer and more appreciative than for almost anything I've done. Nine out of ten of them implied a strong emotional reaction, and that together with the more audible response to the things I hoped were funny, suggested a quite deep involvement during the experience of watching the play. It was never intended only to convey information, but it aimed at exploring the mystery of an exceptional relationship between two exceptional men. I never intended it as a "documentary" and would never claim that it is....

Notes

1. Stephen MacDonald has worked in the theatre as a playwright, director and actor. He was the Artistic Director of Dundee Rep, Edinburgh Royal Lyceum and Leicester Phoenix.

2 MacDonald, Stephen. 1983. *Not About Heroes: The Friendship of Siegfried Sassoon and Wilfred Owen*. London: Faber and Faber.

3 Siegfried Sassoon (1886 – 1967), was educated at Marlborough and Clare College, Cambridge. His life was that of a country squire until he volunteered to fight in the First World War. His poetry and prose reflect his War experience.

4 Wilfred Owen (1893 – 1918). Educated in Liverpool and the Shrewsbury Technical College, he taught English in France from 1913-15, then joined the army. At Craiglockhart War Hospital, where he was treated for shell-shock in 1917, he met poet Siegfried Sassoon, who supported his development as a poet. He died in action a week before the end of World War I.

5 Eric Standidge has worked in theatre for over 25 years. In this time he has directed and produced over 50 productions ranging from Grand Opera to children's theatre touring the very poorest districts of Peru, Columbia, Bolivia and Chile; from London's West End to the Highlands of Scotland and from New York to Moscow. He is a director of General Entertainments Associates, a company specialising in producing and promoting international theatre tours, with offices in London and Amsterdam.

(http://www.playbyplay.co.uk/aboutus.php)

CHAPTER FIVE

THE "COMPOSER PLAYWRIGHT":
DAVID POWNALL

David Pownall[1], author of *Master Class*[2], in an interview with DMD, 4.3.1985

DMD
During the last few years, the number of plays about poets, composers, actors, etc. (in short, artists) has increased considerably. Could you think of an explanation for this remarkable development

DP
I think the artist has always been a part of the theatre's interest: even in *Hamlet* you have players, and in other Jacobean plays you have the figure generally of the actor rather than the artist. It is remarkable that there are so many explorations of what is essentially the artist in society. That has probably something to do with the fact that the artist is feeling increasingly threatened, I think, by an age that is getting beyond his understanding. The artist is so confused himself that he will deal primarily with that confusion before he can actually cope with anybody else's. I think you are dealing with instinct. I mean I don't go about choosing plays consciously. I don't say I'll take this one off the shelf and write about it. Something excites you and pinning down why it is exciting is difficult, but at the moment, playwrights and novelists are very excited by biographies, by writers, by actors, painters. I know that a lot of people are worried about this, especially in America, with all these musicals. I think in a way they started it. I don't believe that it means that people are less interested in ordinary people. I just think that in a way, perhaps, the position of the hero has more and more been taken by the artist, because he is an individual, rather than a movement, and we live in a polarized world, politically polarized. It excites the imagination.

DMD
What excited your imagination to write *Master Class*?

DP
That was very simple in my case. I came upon a transcript of the minutes of the actual Musicians Union Conference in Moscow in January, 1948. A BBC correspondent who was working in Moscow had translated it and edited it and published it in a little thin book[3], and I read just the minutes themselves. They froze your blood on the one hand, but they also made you laugh. There was a kind of mixture of horror and mockery, if you like, and I immediately knew that I wanted to write a play about this. It took me about two years to work out the way of doing it. I just wanted to pass on, if I could, to everyone the emotions I felt when I read the minutes, the predicament of the composers themselves. Also what had prompted the conference, that Stalin did believe that he could control music, that he could get out of the artists what he wanted; he believed that, otherwise he would not have had the conference at all. So it was a very simple, almost mundane beginning.

DMD
What sources did you use?

DP
There were very few, indeed. I shaped the characters really out of their music, Shostakovich and Prokofiev. I had studied Stalin at University, and there was one very good book which I went back to; that was about the extent of my reading. A little bit here and there. I tried to find out things about Zhdanov, it was very difficult. I went to Russia, and I didn't find out very much. Stalin didn't exist. I went to the Kremlin, in January, in the snow, and all I really got from that was a very good impression of the atmosphere of what it was like—as for actually asking, or getting any research done, they didn't even admit they existed.

DMD
What was the cooperation with the director and the actors in *Master Class* like?

DP
Well, that was very, very close. We spent a year casting the play. It is a very difficult play to cast[4]. We worked through hundreds of actors to try to find the right one. They didn't only have to play the piano, but they also, in

the British production, had to be able to act with the piano. That took me a year, and I worked with the director all the time right from the very beginning of the script, auditioning the actors, and trying to get the right people who could credibly be composers on stage and perform at that very high level of acting. So I was deeply involved. Timothy West[5] was the first person we cast, we thought that he would make a very good Stalin. In many ways, he is the easiest to cast, really; the problems are the two composers. There is no doubt that Stalin is the main character in the play, but it is very much an ensemble piece. I tend to write all my plays that once the actor is on stage, he doesn't get off. So there is a quartet or a quintet, who are all on stage all the time, and so they have got to play together.

DMD
How did you like the production in Düsseldorf[6]?

DP
It is very difficult when you don't understand the language; all I could go on was the impression. My impression of the actors was a good impression. The set is very strange, very strange indeed. I think Prokofiev seemed to me to be a very strong actor. As a group, as a quartet, they seemed strong to me, they seemed to play well together. Well, what did you think?

DMD
I thought that Stalin wasn't strong enough in switching from one mood to another. He wasn't dangerous enough.

DP
Well, yes, there have been other productions where the actors have had similar problems. I don't know whether they understood well enough that that is what he was like. The audience should have seen that change, that moment of change. He is unpredictable.

DMD
What did you think of the reviews? B.A. Young [Financial Times] found the play lacking in clear structure.

DP
Now B.A. Young is a very, very old man. His reviews are quite odd. I don't really know precisely what he means. I think maybe what he means

is that he couldn't keep up. That it was hard to find his way back. It related directly to what we were saying: the very swift changes, he couldn't catch up, you know. He likes standing still, progressing gently, rather than with radical and very energetic alterations.

DMD

John Barber [Daily Telegraph] wrote that the main aspect of the play is that you cannot command creativity from an artist.

DP

I think the play is much more than that. The artists generally do not spend any time at all really talking about how they do write their own music. Most of the time they are trying to find a way to survive, to do what Stalin wants them to do. I leave most of that to the audience. They know the way an artist works. I don't think any audience believes that the artists create work by dictation. There is a natural sympathy that all people have. This is one of the things the play is about. But the muse doesn't get discussed a great deal by the two composers, only what Stalin tries to do is replace the muse with himself. Really, it is himself they are going to serve, he is the muse, the inspiration—"do it for me".

DMD

I think that no critic realized that the smashing of the records was not planned but came as a result of Prokofiev mentioning Diaghilev[7].

DP

You are right: I didn't want it to appear, within the play, that he Stalin had brought all those records just to smash them. He hadn't. He brought them there so that he could talk about them, so that he could say: what do you think of this, what do you think of that. The trigger was Diaghilev, and also, by then, to punish Prokofiev, for actually having the dignity to stand up for himself—when Zhdanov insulted him and he walked out and said that he won't be spoken to like that. The trigger is Diaghilev, but it is also to punish Prokofiev for this moment of self-assertion.

DMD

The Guardian wrote that in *Master Class* you show "Stalin the man"...

DP

I accept that. I don't think any playwright tries to write plays about people who are just ideas. You can only write about people, and Stalin was a man, and Zhdanov was a man, and they were composed by their education, their background. I very much wanted them to be human. I mean, not caricatures, political caricatures.

DMD
Do you think that "bio-plays" about artists are an attempt of the dramatist to come to terms with being an artist him/herself by experiencing what it was for someone else to have been an artist?

DP
Yes, I think that is part of it. With regard to *Master Class* it could be: what made me so excited when I read the minutes and what was it that made me know that I wanted to write a play about it. I mean all my plays are not like that, but I have written another play about composers, in 1976, called *Music to Murder By*, which is a biography. You see, I don't think we would be excited by this unless it was actually going to do something for us. In other words, it's to do with the business of being able to see other people's positions in society clearly. I think if you actually haven't got a political doctrine then it is a very confused time for an artist, for all artists.

DMD
Especially since Mrs. Thatcher took over?

DP
No, I don't think she is anything peculiar, but people have been very confused since the war, you know. It's probably something to do with trying to find out what you can do, really, without giving away your independence. A lot of these plays are actually very independent. I don't think a lot of people when they are just starting out for their first plays write about artists

DMD
I think Brenton is a good example of this

DP
Yes. I think you have reached a certain level and you are actually living in London then it is time to. It has something to do with examining your own status, who you are, what you are, what you're doing. There is a lot of pressure today, on writers, on all forms of artists, if you like, to become political, very conscious of everything; that confuses ordinary people, when they face the masses of news and information and causes and

problems that every day hit them. And people can't actually cope with it. It's too much for them, they can't deal with it. Unless they've got a doctrine; then everything gets squeezed into that. With the artist, it is just the same. Trying to keep some kind of balance, some kind of control. He ends up trying to write about people who are akin, or similar.

DMD
In your opinion, what part does suffering play in the artist's life? Is it a prerequisite to good quality in the artist's creation?

DP
I think it's true that for any serious—for want of a better word you have to use the word "quality"—of being able to create and interpret as a writer you are not going to understand it and it's not going to enable you to write plays, novels. I think there are certain types of art, at certain levels, where you can be and just be blissfully happy. As if you had never experienced life at all. Certain art-forms, if you like child-like artists; they almost certainly are suffering, but they are trying to create a kind of heaven for themselves, so it is not himself he has put in there, it's a dream of what he would like.

DMD
Like *Alice in Wonderland*?

DP
That's right. It's the suffering that creates things. The artist is in many ways fortunate that he can do something from suffering, he can use it, whereas the ordinary person doesn't have a lot of facilities of using their suffering. This doesn't mean that all plays, all books, are very dark, very serious.

DMD
I found that in most plays about artists, emotions tend to dominate over the intellect. Please comment.

DP
If you put an artist on the stage, you can legitimately make that artist more emotionally articulate, and the people will accept that. Artists have the reputation of people who are very articulate about their emotions, about what they feel. So once a person comes on stage who is an artist, then he has a licence to be extravagant, about his own self, about his emotions,

whereas if a man with an insurance company acted like that it would be slightly odd. So that's quite useful. It is also a dangerous story, or it can at least be, if it's too easy, so you avoid the insurance man because he is so dull, or he is so reserved, it is much harder to work on this. I think a lot of it has also to do with the whole business of performance and art and popular art and popular music, and the new hero. I don't see our theatres as being separated from popular music. After the war, what has happened is that popular music created a new breed of hero, which was just a singer, and they're idolized to a phenomenal degree. They have, if you like, created the foundation of this new interest in the artist. In general, they are not articulate about this; all that happens is that you get the fans and you get the artists talking about their lives in a kind of newspaper way, in very simple terms. Our interest in the artist and that interest in the artist, I think that is all part of the same thing: a new kind of hero who doesn't actually have to commit heroic deeds. All he's got to show is himself breaking free, expressing something, but it doesn't have to be heroic or good. I mean the man can be good at it, a fiend, a maniac, as long as he's broken out, and making a lot of money. He just doesn't have to go to work like other people go to work. He doesn't lead a dull life, that is enough to make him a hero. That is all part of the same thing. What we are fighting against is uniformity, a developing uniformity, not only in totalitarian countries but throughout the world. Anything that is outside of what the ordinary people are now focusing on. Look at all the kids and what they want. They don't want to be factory workers. They don't want to work in an office. They all want to be pop stars, or they all want to be writers, or actors. Hopeless, of course, because they won't be. That will make them very unhappy and dissatisfied with what they are going to have to do.

DP
I've just written a new play on Ira Aldridge[8]. He was a black American Negro. A Shakespearean actor in the 1820s. He came to England. Did all the great roles, Lear, Hamlet, Macbeth, Shylock. Black actors can't do that now! They can do Othello. He worked in England, toured all around Britain. They wouldn't let him into the West End. Now don't forget this was in 1825. He was a highly political man. Within himself he was just an actor. Because he was black, because he was an American black— obviously from a slavery background—he had a political charisma. From England he went to France, Germany, performed in Berlin, was decorated by the King. Then he went to Russia. He finally died in Poland. Quite an amazing man, an astonishing man. This is a very intersecting case. The story was brought to me by a very fine black actor[9], whom I had written

two parts for before; he brought me the story, because he thinks he is
Aldridge reincarnated. He's serious; he had a drawing, an etching of him.
We've worked on this for five years. I've just finished writing it. This is a
play about an actor, a play about an actor who is a black man, coming to
play Shakespeare who was a white man, it's about revolutionary Europe,
and it's set in Poland. The action of the play takes place in one day in a
real town in eastern Poland.

DMD
Among those plays, a large number are "one-person-shows" or two-
handers. Do you think this is only because of financial/commercial
reasons?

DP
We live in an age in which—since I have been writing, that's all I know
about it (before that I was in industry)—I automatically write for small
casts. If you asked me to write a play with 12 people in it I don't think I'd
know where to start. I all my plays the actors are used all the time. I can't
waste them. To be totally frank, the primary motivation for one-man
shows is that it's highly mobile, and there is hardly any set. I love one-
man plays, I've written two, one for a woman and one for a man; as a
writing exercise it's very, very exciting and good for me. And one person
on the stage can't do much, really. He can make a phone call, he can take
his clothes off, he can sit down, go and read a notebook, but there is no
action, it's all talk, all words and the audience have to listen, because
otherwise there is no point of going. They know before they go that it is
going to be no active play and the problem for most playwrights is to get
people to listen.

Notes

1. David Pownall was born in Liverpool in 1938. He had decided by the age of 15
that he was going to be a writer. He studied English and History at Keele
University, graduating in 1960 and worked as a personnel officer with the Ford
Motor Company. In 1963 he went to Northern Rhodesia (now Zambia) and was
employed in the copper-mining industry. During the six years he spent in Africa he
started writing plays for the co-operative theatres in the mining towns. In 1969 he
returned to England to write for a living. First, he worked with the Century Mobile
Theatre in the north-west which produced his first play in the U.K. – *How To
Grow A Guerrilla;* then moved with the company to the Duke's Playhouse,
Lancaster where he was the resident writer from 1971-6. His plays from this period
include *Little Jimmy Williamson, Buck Ruxton,* and *A Tale Of Two Town Halls.* In

1975, together with Edward Adams as director, he started Paines Plough, a touring theatre company which was to specialise in new plays. During the next two years he wrote exclusively for this group, producing *Crates On Barrels, Ladybird, Ladybird, Music To Murder By, Motorcar* and *Richard III Part Two*. The last two plays were staged at the National Theatre (Cottesloe), in December 1977. From his African experiences came the much-acclaimed pair of comic novels, *The Raining Tree War,* and *African Horse,* (Faber, paperback edition in Penguin). A collection of short stories *My Organic Uncle* (Faber) was published in 1976, followed by another comic novel, *God Perkins* in 1977. Another novel, *Light On A Honeycomb* was published in 1978. His plays for children are *The Dream Of Chief Crazy Horse* (Faber), and *Blue Genes.* He has also written for radio and television.

2 Pownall, David. 1983. *Master Class*. London: Faber and Faber.

3 Werth, Alexander. *Musical Uproar in Moscow.* London: Turnstile, 1949.

4 Timothy West played Stalin, Peter Kelly played Prokofiev, David Bamber played Shostakovich and Jonathan Adams played Zhdanov. The production was directed by Justin Greene. Following its premiere at the Leicester Haymarket in January 1983, the production ran at the Old Vic in London from 18 January to 25 February 1984, then transferred to the Wyndham's Theatre in the West End from 29 February to 7 April, 1984.

5 See interview with Timothy West in Chapter Seven of this book.

6 The first German language production of *Master Class* premiered at the Düssedorfer Schauspielhaus in November 1984 with Wolfgang Reinbacher as Stalin, Karlheinz Vietsch as Prokofiev, Bert Oberdorfer as Shostakovich and Dieter Prochnow as Zhdanov. The production was directed by Rolf Stahl.

7 Sergei Pavlovich Diaghilev (1872-1929), Russian impresario.

8 David Pownall, *Black Star*, in *Pownall: Plays 2*. London: Oberon Books, 2001.

9 Joseph Marcell. See details about this actor on his website: http://josephmarcell.com/

CHAPTER SIX

PIANO AND PROKOFIEV: PETER KELLY

Peter Kelly[1] played composer Sergei Prokofiev[2] in David Pownall's *Master Class*[3]. Interview with DMD on 25.3.1985.

DMD
During the last few years, the number of plays about poets, composers, actors, etc. (in short, artists) has increased considerably. Could you think of an explanation for this remarkable development

PK
Yes, that is true, there was, for example, *Total Eclipse*[4], and there were other plays like that. I suppose there is always a great interest in the works of the artist, how he arrives at a situation where he is able to create an extraordinary, new and interesting work: is this because of his life or is he born with it? When I started work on Prokofiev, of course I read biographies about him. None of them really contradicted each other, though some were from a Soviet point of view, and some from a Western point of view. The Western books said that when he went back he didn't write anything decent, and vice versa from the Soviets, but as far as he, the man, was concerned there were no contradictions there. He seemed to have been a thorough professional who would do anything rather than sacrifice his work. I don't really think he compromised when he went back to the Soviet Union, which is a lot for Western people to believe. I think he wrote some wonderful stuff when he came back; perhaps he talked his way round the complaints that he had. I met his son, which was quite helpful, but I did not meet him until after we had opened in Leicester, and he said what I had captured myself, and what the play had captured, was the essence of the man, his enormous pride, his fastidiousness, his amazing dignity. Everything that I discovered in my research on Prokofiev after I had read the script I found was all in the part, it was all there; so I

assumed that David Pownall, who had written it, had obviously done tremendous, thorough research, and I said to him: what books did you read. And he said: "O well, I read one biography, so the basic things I just got out of the music". That says a lot for David's reception.

Prokofiev was a fascinating character to play because the more I have been into the music you could see the character there, it was tremendous, very cerebral, his music is very cerebral, and yet it is based in a kind of Russian folk-music, as well, so he obviously was a man of great passion for his country. I find it quiet as well, with a lot of humorous passages, sarcasms: for example, the first of his accomplished piano pieces is really a kind of turning music up on its head, for his time. From all that wit and sense of humour I get the impression that he was quite a sharp man, fascinating.

DMD
Please describe any cooperation with Pownall during rehearsals.

PK
It was complete, he was at rehearsals practically every day. Because it was a new play, and because that is the way he likes to work. Whenever problems arise, you can discuss it and if it requires a change, you can change it. He is a very adaptable playwright.

DMD
Have you found any particular difficulties in playing the part, and if so, how did you master them?

PK
I suppose that the most difficult was the physical aspect, which, in fact, was exaggerated in the play, for dramatic purposes. I mean Prokofiev was very ill at that time, and if he had been called in by Stalin at that time, he would not have been at his fittest. But at the same time I was helped by the dignity, something which showed the fragility of the man in this condition, but with this tremendous strength of character and belief in his work.

DMD
What did you think of the reviews?

PK
I liked the good ones. Some of them said that it didn't get anywhere, that it entered a highly dramatic situation and didn't develop it. I disagree. I think

they were looking for a blacker picture of Stalin than David [Pownall] presented of this fairly awful man. But at the same time David also wanted to show his kind of weird humanity, he obviously had warm moments as well. And to paint him completely black would have been like a cardboard cutout. I think it is a very clever play.

DMD
How did you get to know Prokofiev's son?

PK
Quite by accident. We were doing the show in Leicester, where it had opened and had been running for a couple of weeks, and after the show one night there was a knock at my door and this very tall, distinguished man was there, and he said: "Good evening, you don't know me, my name is Prokofiev. You've just played my father". I almost kissed his hand and knelt. He was very happy with the way it was portrayed and he told me some stories about the time when he was a child, how tough things were with money when Prokofiev had trouble with the authorities, how he did manage to pay his bills and that kind of thing.

DMD
Is he a musician, too?

PK
No, he is a painter, and a sculptor, he lives near Greenwich, married to an Englishwoman, three children, they've just had twins.

DMD
Among those plays, a large number are "one-person-shows" or two-handers. Do you think this is only because of financial or commercial reasons?

PK
Yes, I do, because I have done three one-man-shows in my time, though not about artists. Well, it is an enormous challenge for the actor to stand up and say he is so and so, or whatever, and you are lucky if you can get a very clever writer, who can delve deeply into the character, events in his life, which shaped the character. You always have to remember, of course, that you are presenting a theatrical piece, and therefore it has to be entertaining as well as interesting, informative and true. But I do think this is valid. I think people are fascinated to imagine what people, these artists,

must be like. I mean, *Total Eclipse*, which I mentioned earlier, which is about these poets, Rimbaud and Verlaine, was fascinating, I think, because not many people knew about their type of life, and people are always interested to know what they were really like. What was Picasso really like, what was Tchaikovsky really like. I think he'd be a very interesting one-man show, if you have someone who can play the piano well enough. I mean the cast in *Master Class* was limited by the fact that Pownall needed people who could play the piano reasonably well. In fact, he stumbled on me quite by chance. I had been in a play of his and he did not know I could play the piano. He just didn't know, it never cropped up. And then he said to a friend of mine: Peter would be good for the part, what a shame he can't play the piano. And this friend of mine said: but he does play the piano.

DMD
And now everybody knows.

PK
And now most people know. As soon as Liubimov[5] saw it he said: "Right, that is Lyamshin", which is rather unfortunate because it is not an enormous, wonderfully exciting part. Nevertheless...

DMD
Do you think that "bio-plays" about artists are an attempt of the dramatist to come to terms with being an artist him/herself by experiencing what it was for someone else to have been an artist?

PK
Yes. I think they obviously sympathize with them and their struggle. I mean David very clearly related this struggle against the state with the struggle against the Arts Council cuts. It is not easy for a writer in this country to earn a living. You have to be very successful and write some enormously successful play, or a screenplay; otherwise, just to be a sort of day-to-day playwright doing plays that are done at fringe theatres—you don't get paid very much and it is a hard and lonely life. So I think that they find it very easy to relate to an artist; and what they admire most about the artist is this enormous strength to carry on in spite of everything: enormous illness, ill health. Prokofiev, you know, was only allowed to compose for half an hour a day; everything was sacrificed for that half hour. That was important. He had to squeeze the last of creativity out of him before he died. And he knew that that was it. He also felt that it was

his duty to do that, his duty to his gift, if you like. I also think that in this country, in Britain, unless you are a painter or a musician, people like actors and writers, they seldom call themselves artists, because it sounds a bit grand. I think that is a mistake, because the minute you recognize that you are an artist, you realize that you do have a duty to your talent, whatever it is.

DMD
In your opinion, what part does suffering play in the artist's life? Is it a prerequisite to good quality in the artist's creation?

PK
I don't think it is necessary. It depends on the individual. Did Picasso suffer very much? I don't think so. It did not stop him from producing a great many works of art. I think that sometimes people are in unfortunate circumstances when starting out. The fact that they overcome those odds again shows the strength of their gift, everything is sacrificed for that.

DMD
What do you think is the artist's relation to emotions?

PK
An artist obviously does work from the heart; but at the same time the head is very important because of the technique and the discipline that are required, although that is not true of every artist. The best ones have both. They certainly have an easier life if they can have both. Tchaikovsky obviously did not. He was not very practical, and he was a very miserable and unhappy man. Van Gogh as well. But someone like Picasso was almost commercially oriented, and in fact so was Prokofiev, you know, he was for ever salvaging bits and pieces from works that were not being performed very much; like bits of his symphonies were used in ballet. So I do not think it is necessary, suffering. The situation in Britain, with the theatre, it is a struggle, it is not easy to get work, too many actors and not enough work. Whether that is the reason why we have got a better system or a better standard of acting, I do not know, than in other countries where there is more subsidy, backing, like in Germany, where there is enormous subsidy for the theatre. But the standard, I am told, is not wonderful. Italy is the same, too: really very well supported, and from what I hear the standard of the theatre there is not very good. My only other experience is Holland. Again, it is very well supported, you're guaranteed a job before you leave drama school, otherwise you do not do your last year. So there

is no struggle, to feel that this job is desperately important because it is a matter of life and death.

DMD
How would you define the message of *Master Class*?

PK
It was a fictitious situation, but it was not, in a sense; that what happened in that room happened to them in the Soviet Union. I always felt that Prokofiev had to win, at all costs. And I believe that he did. Because he showed Stalin that you cannot write music to order. He said: "Alright, you want this terrible folk song, you want this lalala, there you are, that's it". And Stalin obviously realized that it was a non-starter, and there was nothing he could do about it. So what he said was a very mild: "Please, please help me, do something. I've killed all these people in the war, you have got to start and make them proud of their country again and believe in the government". Which is dangerous. You cannot do that. I mean Shostakovich[5] had a much more difficult time than Prokofiev. Prokofiev was older, Shostakovich was then in the middle of all that Stalin thing, and although he had hardly been to the West he was an official representative of Soviet society.

Notes

1 Peter Kelly is from Scotland, where he performed at the Citizens' Theatre, Glasgow and at the Traverse Theatre, Edinburgh. Theatre work includes *Crime and Punishment*, directed by Yuri Liubimov, at the Lyric Hammersmith (1983). He also works in TV, radio and film.
2 Sergei Prokofiev (1891-1956), Russian composer.
3 Pownall, David. 1983. *Master Class*. London: Faber and Faber.
4 The main characters of *Total Eclipse* by Christopher Hampton are French poets Paul Verlaine (1844-1896) and Arthur Rimbaud (1854-1891.
5 Yuri Liubimov (b. 1917—) Russian theatre director, One of his most rebellious productions was *Hamlet* (1970), showing Russia, and not Denmark, as a prison. Other classic productions include Bulgakov's *Master i Margarita* (*Master and Margarita*), Pushkin's *Boris Godunov*, Pasternak's *Zhivago*, and Mozhayev's *Zhivoi* (*Alive*), about the destruction of Russian peasantry by Bolsheviks. (Meyer-Dinkgräfe 2002, 179-180)
6 Dimitri Shostakovich (1906-1975), Russian composer.

CHAPTER SEVEN

STALIN AND BEECHAM:
TIMOTHY WEST

Timothy West[1] played Stalin[2] in David Pownall's[3] *Master Class*[4] and Sir Thomas Beecham[5] in *Beecham*[6] by Caryl Brahms and Ned Sherrin. Interview with DMD on 14.3.1985

DMD
During the last few years, the number of plays about poets, composers, actors, etc. (in short, artists) has increased considerably. Could you think of an explanation for this remarkable development?

TW
I do not know. I believe that it is very difficult to write a satisfactory play about a creative artist. I think that normally plays about writers, dramatists, composers, painters and so on do not really work because you cannot write a play about what people *do*, you can only write a play about what they *are*. But it seems that recently there have been more plays about *interpretative* artists. I think they serve to identify a particular kind of historical and cultural period in people's minds. Therefore you can bring in many other social and political overtones. *Master Class* is a very unusual play, because it is not, in any sense, a portrait of Prokofiev[7], or Shostakovich[8], or Zhdanov[9], or Stalin. It is more the kind of play that Shaw might have written, with four people inhabiting a play of argument, and those people are there to embody the kind of ideas and the kind of convictions and standpoints that those people might broadly be imagined to have had. So that the Stalin I played in *Master Class* is not the real Stalin any more than Shaw's Saint Joan was the real Saint. Joan, or Shakespeare's Richard II was the real Richard II.

DMD
But that was different in the case of *Beecham*?

TW

Yes. *Beecham* is not really a play at all. It is a portrait, an affectionate portrait, a celebration, if you like, of a distinctive man. I don't think there would have been any reason to do it at all had it not been a fact that Beecham is largely regarded by many people as just a lot of funny stories. Indeed, he was of course a very witty and devastating man, but he also had an extraordinary love and interest in, and passionate regard for the welfare of music. The play, the evening, the piece, whatever you call it, does treat with the conductor/impresario as well as the joker.

DMD

Among those plays, a large number are "one-person-shows" or two-handers. Do you think this is only because of financial/commercial reasons?

TW

I think so, largely. We know that the general public react most favourably to large-scale plays, plays with big production values. But nowadays if you are an unknown author and come up with a play with more than five or six people in it, you will be very lucky to get it shown, by a commercial management anyway.

DMD

You played the characters of Stalin and Beecham. How did you prepare for the portrayal of those characters?

TW

I seem to have got stuck with playing real people. I do not know why it is, I have not sought it, but it has kind of happened. My usual practice is to do quite a lot of research, aware at the same time that you are playing not the person but the author's concept of the person, and therefore a lot of research that you do will be irrelevant and sometimes even confusing, and will have to be thrown out of the window. I still think that it is as well to have done it, though, it builds up your off-stage existence in a way which I find very helpful.

DMD

Could you give some details of your research?

TW

When you are talking about people within living memory the opportunities for research are much greater, but then the responsibilities to be accurate are greater, too. Clearly, if you are operating in the historical era of photographs you've got a lot going for you as far as physical resemblance is concerned, but then you also have a lot to live up to because everybody else would have seen that photograph as well. Stalin didn't like being filmed, so there is not much cinema footage to work with here. He accepted it as a necessity of office but didn't actually court publicity of that sort. On the footage that does exist, though, you begin to see a lot more of the person in action. Sometimes you are lucky enough to see him in an unguarded moment: you learn an awful lot from a person in repose when he doesn't know he is being watched. Film is very helpful in that sense. Photographs, of course, recordings, sound recordings are useful. Biographical memories you have to treat with caution because so many of them are contradictory. I played our King Edward VII, years ago, he was king from 1900-1910; and when I did it there were still a few people around who had known him as children. Their descriptions of his voice varied enormously. Some said he had a deep voice with a strong guttural German accent, others said there was no trace of a German diaect. You just can't trust any biography not to be subjective.

DMD

Have you found any particular difficulties in playing Stalin or Beecham, and if so, how did you master them?

TW

I didn't find any difficulties with Beecham, except those that I could solve by simply working harder at it. Stalin was very difficult because he was a person who was deliberately wayward and capricious and enjoyed wrong-footing people. I talked to a man in the War Office who during the war had been in charge of liaison with Moscow. He talked to Stalin quite a lot, his Russian was obviously very good, on the telephone. He would begin a formal introduction: "How are you, comrade Stalin", and there would suddenly be this terrible silence. He would think he had said something wrong. And then suddenly Stalin would be tremendously jocular and would start telling this man a funny story, but of which the humour was absolutely incomprehensible. You could not see where it was meant to be funny. And so of course the poor man would fail to laugh, and immediate offence would be taken. He was certain that Stalin had done all this deliberately. If you are playing somebody like that, of course it is very difficult because you have got to dig beneath that behaviour, you have got to uncover the real desires which have motivated this action at a fundamental level. We talk glibly about the basic rule that as an actor, even if you intellectually disapprove of the person you play, you have to identify with them when you are playing them You can't just *comment* on objectionable people like Hitler, or Idi Amin, or Mrs Thatcher; you have to see things from their point of view. You have to find the terms in which he or she would have justified the appalling things which they knew they had done. Otherwise the performance is not going to be believable.

DMD
Please describe any kind of cooperation with the author, David Pownall, during rehearsals for *Master Class*

TW
There was a very strong cooperation, and he is a wonderful author to work with on a play, because he is never intrusive but does like to sit in on early rehearsals. He has a good ear for listening to what you are doing and conditioning it with what he knows what will inevitably happen to the thing during the course of rehearsals. He doesn't say, like some playwrights do (fortunately very few): "No, no, you can't do it like that", to which one has to reply: "Give us a chance, we still have four weeks of rehearsal". David knows approximately how it's finally going to come out; he has worked in the theatre for most of his life. He will also appreciate that there are moments that you will never be able to get right: "I don't understand what makes me say that at that particular point in the scene?" and that perhaps this might be because he could have written it better. He had great respect for the director and for the four actors, and it was a very happy working relationship.

DMD
I think the text also helps to express Stalin's swift changes of mood.

TW
Yes, that's right.

DMD
What was the cooperation like in case of *Beecham*?

TW

Oh, splendid. *Beecham* we really put together during a fortnight, the director, and Terry Wale, who performs it with me. The three of us lived in one house in Salisbury where we were originally rehearsing it. We only had a fortnight to rehearse it, we were all involved in other things. So we did it on the basis of this rather bald script – no disrespect the two authors; they said, well, look, you are going to find things about the character, about the show, that might make you want to change things or juggle things around. Therefore we were not presented with a finished script. The three of us talked about it at breakfast, while walking over the fields to the theatre to rehearse; we talked about it at lunch, and in the evenings over dinner, and we managed to put it together. In a funny way that is something you could never do in London, because one of you is probably living in Highgate, the other in Wimbledon, the director in Ealing, so you don't see each other except during working hours. If you can actually give 17 to 18 hours a day to a project, it's amazing what you can accomplish.

DMD

Do you think that "bio-plays" about artists are an attempt of the dramatist to come to terms with being an artist him/herself by experiencing what it was for someone else to have been an artist?

TW

Yes, that is an interesting suggestion and I think it may to a certain extent be true. I don't think it quite works, though. If you get involved in writing about somebody else's creative process, it is of no real interest to the general public. You can't write a play about Beethoven: gosh, look, he worked hard on his 7th symphony, and then he wrote it, and it was terrific! In an extraordinary way, Mozart, who is used a lot by Peter Shaffer[10] in *Amadeus*, almost goes as far as breaking that rule because you only have to play the music to have people say: unquestionably that is genius. You do not have to know anything about him at all, but when you say that you sat down and heard that noise, we know pretty well what you might have felt. But there are not very many people about whom you can say that. You can't say it about Shakespeare; you cannot produce 20 lines of iambic pentameter in his best style and expect people to know what you are on about because it just doesn't work as twice-cooked meat. I think you are right, some writers do like to produce plays about the creative process, but they tend not to engage the general public. What is interesting about *Master Class* is that you see the creative process not as the kind of driving force of the play, but you see it defined by the political arguments that are placed to obstruct it, don't you? That's what makes it a fascinating play.

DMD
In your opinion, what part does suffering play in the artist's life? Is it a prerequisite to good quality in the artist's creation?

TW
I think it is a Romantic cliché. It is all a question of personality, isn't it? You could point to certain artists who have been pushed to greater and greater efforts and to more deeply felt works as they suffered; and indeed you could point to nations who have given birth to great art because they have always been in a state of peril and turmoil, whereas other nations who've enjoyed a peaceful existence and don't suffer, tend not produce much. I think it is very dangerous to take this as any kind of rule. After all, Rossini had an extremely comfortable life: towards the end of his life he was writing in bed, and if a piece of manuscript fluttered out of his reach he would rewrite from memory rather than take the trouble of getting out of bed to retrieve it.

DMD
What do you think is the artist's relation to emotions?

TW
Emotions that are generated by the protagonist are very personal. People can understand intellectual arguments, they can apply them to what is going on in the play, with understanding and identification. Emotion, though, is very personal. If you make your leading character behave entirely according to these emotional drives, whims if you like, first of all you get only the author's word that that's how he does react. Secondly, you might feel as a member of the audience that that is not the way you yourself would react in such a situation and therefore you cannot totally identify with that person.

DMD
Could you comment on the critical response to *Master Class* and *Beecham*?

TW
I think what people said about *Beecham* was fairly predictable: a lot of them found it completely lovely, and that was very nice. Others found it

slightly trivial. With *Master Class*, which I think was rather a major play, I was surprised and disappointed that one or two people – not many, the general tone of the notices was very good – complained that this was not a real portrait, not historically true.

DMD
But that is obvious from the start, isn't it?

TW
Yes. I would have thought it was quite clear from five minutes into the play that it was not supposed to be an accurate chronicle. People, I think, must have had a very difficult evening if that was what they were expecting: the four characters never in fact met as a group. Another criticism was that during the composition scene in Act II the play went off to in different kind of direction. I think in strictly "How to Write a Play, Chapter One" terms, it probably did. But it didn't seem to me to be a worry. I felt the play did get back on to its level of danger immediately afterwards, and the sequence itself, I thought, was brilliantly funny. Composition by committee.

DMD
When I saw the play at Wyndham's, I thought that that scene was just a prolonged kind of whim of Stalin.

TW
Absolutely right, yes. I mean the fact that it did go on so long, that it was taken so seriously, was part of the nature of that whim, really.

DMD
In the play, Stalin says that he had to give up all his family life for the nation. What do you think about such a statement?

TW
It is very difficult to know, because Stalin was very practised at deluding himself. I have absolutely no doubt that he felt that, from time to time. Whether it was an objective statement of truth, I don't know. That seems to me irrelevant. What is important is that he thought it was true.

DMD
I read in the Daily Mail that you conducted the Royal Philharmonic Orchestra. What was it like?

TW

That is true, and I did that again the other night at the Barbican. It was wonderful. I did not lose them at all the second time, I'm getting better! I am very fond of music and I read music and I sing a little. I had to learn to conduct for a film about Wagner a long time ago. I was taught by one of the Sadler's Wells conductors, and I got a taste for it – I mean one knows the rudiments but I think I had a sort of feel for it. I am very sensible to different interpretations of the same piece, and perhaps while studying the man I have been able to feel what Beecham might have done with this or that bit of music. I hope so.

Notes

1 Timothy West was born in Bradford in 1934, the son of actor Lockwood West. Seasons in repertory in Wimbledon, Newquay, Hull, Northampton, Worthing and Salisbury, coming to the Piccadilly Theatre in the farce *Caught Napping* in 1959. Since then his performances on the London stage have included *Gentle Jack*, *The Trigon*, *The Italian Girl*, *Abelard and Heloise*, *Exiles*, *The Constant Couple*, *Laughter*, *The Homecoming*, *Beecham*, *Master Class*, *The War at Home*, *When We Are Married*, *The Sneeze*, *Long Day's Journey Into Night*, *It's Ralph* and *Twelve Angry Men*. With the Royal Shakespeare Company he first appeared in 1962 in *Nil Carborundum* and *Afore Night Come* at the Arts Theatre, and in seasons at the Aldwych and Stratford until 1966; then in 1975 *Hedda Gabler* (also touring Australia, Canada and the USA). For the Prospect Theatre Company, in the UK and abroad, he has played King Lear, Prospero, Holofernes, Claudius, Enobarbus, Shylock, Bolingbroke in *Richard II* and Mortimer in *Edward II*, as well as Shpigelsky in *A Month in the Country*, Emerson in *A Room with a View* and Samuel Johnson in two plays about the great man. For the Bristol Old Vic company: the musical *Trelawny*, Falstaff in both parts of *Henry IV*, Sartorius in *Widower's Houses*, Solness in *The Master Builder*, Lord Ogleby in *The Clandestine Marriage* and Vanya in *Uncle Vanca*. More recently he has played *King Lear* in Dublin, *Death of a Salesman* and *Macbeth* for Theatr Clwyd, Brian Phelan's *Himself* on tour for the Nuffield Theatre, Southampton, *The Rivals* at Chichester, *Mail order Bride* and *Getting On* at the West Yorkshire Playhouse, Falstaff again for English Touring Theatre, Gloucester in *King lear* at the National Theatre; *The Birthday Party* at the Salisbury Playhouse, on tour and at the Piccadilly Theatre, *The Master Builder* on tour for English Touring Theatre, *Luther* at the National Theatre and the title role in *King Lear* for English Touring Theatre on tour and for a season at the Old Vic. Most recently, he has played *Galileo* for Birmingham Rep., *The Old Country* at the Trafalgar Studios, *A Number* at Sheffield and Menenius in *Coriolanus* for the RSC. In addition, he has numerous major television appearances to his credit, most recently Sir Lester Dedlock for the BBC's *Bleak House*. His book *I'm Here I Think, Where are You?* is published by Coronet, and his autobiography *A Moment Towards the End of the*

Play is published by Nick Hern Books. In 1984 he was made CBE for his services
to the profession.
(http://www.gavinbarkerassociates.co.uk/html/timothy_west.htm)
2 Josef [Iosif Vissarinovich] Stalin (1878-1953), leader of the Soviet Union from
the mid-1920s until his death.
3 See interview with David Pownall in chapter five of this book.
4 Pownall, David. 1983. *Master Class*. London: Faber and Faber.
5 Brahms, Caryl and Ned Sherin, *Beecham*, Playscrips 899.
6 Thomas Beecham (1879-1961), British conductor, founder of several orchestras,
including the London Philharmonic Orchestra and the Royal Philharmonic
Orchestra.
7 Sergei Prokofiev (1891-1956), Russian composer.
8 Dimitri Shostakovich (1906-1975), Russian composer.
9 Andrei Zhdanov (1896-1948), Stalinist politician, responsible for state
censorship of the arts.
10 Peter Shaffer (b. 926), British dramatist, whose main successes include *The
Royal Hunt of the Sun*, *Equus* and *Amadeus*.

CHAPTER EIGHT

ONE PERSON'S GEORGE ELIOT: MARGARET WOLFIT

Margaret Wolfit[1] wrote and performed a one-woman show about George Eliot[2]; Interview with DMD, 26.3.85

DMD
During the last few years, the number of plays about poets, composers, actors, etc. (in short, artists) has increased considerably. Could you think of an explanation for this remarkable development?

MW
I started with an adaptation of George Eliot's novel *The Mill on the Floss* . From that work developed the biographical piece on George Eliot. It premiered in 1978, at the Lyric Hammersmith, and the Soho Poly, and since then I have performed it all over the place, even at universities in the States. I think one of the reasons for the rise of the number of these plays is economic, certainly as far as the one-person show is concerned. A lot of people want to work, and they don't get any, so they create their own. It is a question of practicing your craft. As far as the actual artists' lives are concerned, well, it was very interesting to know about their lives. I was attracted to George Eliot by an interest in her work. That goes back to childhood days: I remember doing excerpts at school. I discovered a letter that I had written to my mother saying I have just been reading a lot of George Eliot. She was somewhat neglected: people were put off by her intellectual aura that made her intimidating. I wanted to see what the woman behind this image was like. I was also fascinated by the works of literature she read as a child. I have a very strong feeling that this reading would influence her way of writing. In her writing she is very demanding, it has a breadth about it that fits in with the kind of literature she read.

DMD
Could you describe your research and the procedure of writing?

MW
I decided to go through a lot of the literature which she read as a child. That was very illuminating about her. I read many biographies on George Eliot. Then I read her letters. One is continually increasing one's knowledge. I would never say I know everything now, and stop. Somebody else would write a book and show another aspect. Then I decided to do it in the first person, to do it as her. So I started with her childhood, selecting various basic things. I went to see one of George Eliot's biographers in the States. He has become a very good friend. In fact, I did originally show him a rough draft of this programme and he had much to comment on it, from which I learnt a lot. One of the things that I discovered which I found fascinating was an Aesop fable on brother and sister, which seemed to be—for me—an extraordinary thing for her to have read as a child. And I put this to him. He wrote back that she could never have read that in her childhood. I think it intrigued him because he went to some library or other to look for himself, and he actually wrote and said that she could have read that fable after all, as it was published at that time. I was very pleased.

DMD
Did you use George Eliot's own words?

MW
I certainly haven't used my own words in my adaptation of *The Mill on the Floss*. Most of what was written was hers.

DMD
Did you have a director for the George Eliot show?

MW
Yes. I think you need another eye, to tell you what is right and what is wrong about it. I had two directors for *The Mill on the Floss* simply because I first did it a long time ago. For the second time I actually had the director who also did the George Eliot biography with me. He is very, very interested in George Eliot. It is good to work with someone who has got the same sort of attitude.

DMD
What made you choose the Purcell Room as a venue?

MW
I took it there, actually, because at that time it was quite cheap. I was testing out the ground, you don't know what your audience is going to be. Somebody like the Brontes are somehow more immediately romantic. George Eliot was plain, she wasn't beautiful, you have to look deeply to find the interest in her. She is a quite hard one to sell, compared with Jane Austen or the Brontes.

DMD
How long did the actual performance of the biographical show last?

MW
When I did it at the Soho Poly I did a shortened version, an hour-version. When I did it at the Purcell Room, it was full-length, you know, two parts with an interval. I have done it in the States, last Easter. I did it at Brown University, and it was full packed. And at Smith College, that was very full. It always depends, at some places you only have got an hour—you have to adapt it. Did you see *Beecham*[3]?

DMD
Yes, and I interviewed Timothy West[4].

MW
Oh. did you. It didn't have a long run. We were talking about it and I said to him [T. West]: "This could be put on again at another time, and you'll suddenly find it would work." Theatre is such an extraordinary animal, you just never know. When I did that George Eliot biographical at the Soho Poly, I was personally rather low, after losing my mother. I didn't get the audience. I think it was the wrong venue, but I had the feeling, very strongly, that if I did it again, in another way, at another place, it might be successful.

DMD
Do you think that biographical plays about an artist are an attempt of the dramatist to come to terms with being an artist him/herself?

MW

Yes, I imagine any kind of writing teaches you about yourself. Whatever the artist's field is, there is something that is universal. You recognize in a writer something about yourself as an actress. One is drawn to certain people. A few years ago, after I had done much work on George Eliot, I felt I must get away from her; I must do something other than a writer. I was trying to think of other people. I was walking on the road and the name of Octavia Hill[5] came to my head. At the time that came into my head I was thinking that she was involved in some way with photography. When I began to research into this person I discovered that she was in fact linked by marriage to George Eliot. That was fascinating because I had thought I was getting away from George Eliot and in fact I wasn't getting away from her at all. Then I discovered that she had lived in Hampstead and was deeply interested in saving the Swiss Cottage Fields from being built over to keep them for poor people—they are now built over. This is where I spent a lot of my life. In some way you begin to think "What's going on, there's something in the ether that draws you to people".

DMD

What do you think is the relation between artists and emotions?

MW

In George Eliot's case, she was both emotional and intellectual. I do not see why you have to divorce the two. Emotion is energy. Sometimes your emotions are inhibited, and you may be intellectually superior. In the theatre, you are dealing with both. George Eliot was a very emotional woman, but she was also an intellectual, very much so. I think for a play to be wholly successful it needs to be a marriage of the two things. I don't think I consciously set out to say, well, this has got to be emotional.

DMD

What part does suffering play in the artist's life?

MW

If you are an artist, you have an added sensitivity. If you have an added sensitivity, you are going to suffer more than other people. We are talking about the artist, therefore we are talking about what the qualities of the artist are. If you are an artist, then you have an added sensitivity, which is a very painful thing to have.

Notes

1 Margaret Wolfit is the daughter of Sir Donald Wolfit (1902-1968).

2 *George Eliot* was the pen name of English novelist Mary Ann Evans (1819-1880)

3 Thomas Beecham (1879-1961), British conductor, founder of several orchestras, including the London Philharmonic Orchestra and the Royal Philharmonic Orchestra.

4 Timothy West (b. 1934), British actor. See interview with West in chapter seven of this book.

5 Octavia Hill (1838-1912) was an English social reformer.

CHAPTER NINE

PLAYING THE NON-GENIUS:
TOM WILKINSON AND T.S. ELIOT

Tom Wilkinson[1] played T.S. Eliot[2] in the original London production of Michael Hastings'[3] *Tom and Viv*[4]. Interview with DMD, 29.3.1985. The play was later revived, on Broadway and London, with Ed Hermann[5] as T.S.Eliot.

DMD
During the last few years, the number of plays about poets, composers, actors, etc. (in short, artists) has increased considerably. Could you think of an explanation for this remarkable development?

TW
Yes, I have an attractive notion about this. E.P.Thompson[6] is a major spokesman and theorist of nuclear disarmament in this country. He was saying that this country had not always been the country of bullies: that it is also the country of poets. There are two Britains, and at the moment that Thatcherite bully seems to have taken over the whole of people's lives, the whole of their thinking, and it is not surprising to me that people then turn towards poets. It is the exact antithesis of Thatcherite right wing brutalism. It does not surprise me that there is an upsurge of interest in that problem. There does not really seem to be a way forward at the moment, the left seems to be in some disarray, and the right is very much in the preponderance all over the world.

DMD
How did you prepare for the part of T.S.Eliot?

TW
Max Stafford Clark is the director of the Royal Court, and the director of *Tom and Viv*. He is very meticulous and he insists on a great amount of

meticulousness from his actors. First of all, I was quite familiar with
T.S.Eliot as a teenager, he was a hero of mine, and even at that time I had
got some a record of T.S.Eliot reading *The Waste Land*. In my twenties
and up until I started doing this play I rather neglected my interest in him.
I did some general research, reread his poems, and read very few
biographical pieces on him; he is a very closed-in man and didn't really
want biographies written. So it was very difficult. The difficulty was to
link your knowledge of Eliot, the sound of his voice, what you think he
was like, and the demands of the play. I found one of the most frustrating
problems about the play was that you saw him as a repressed and
repressive person with lots of problems. He was rather crude. I knew that
that wasn't the entire story of T.S.Eliot and that was very frustrating. He is
one of the towering geniuses of the 20th century and there is no evidence
in the play to suggest that he was anything other than a curious pervert. So
that was a problem. Throughout rehearsals these two things were weighing
on my mind: the demands of the play and what I felt were the demands of
the real person. I made a very unhappy compromise until very late in the
day when two things happened: Michael Hastings is a friend of Peter
Ackroyd[8] who wrote the recent biography of T.S.Eliot, and he came to talk
about T.S.Eliot. He didn't tell me anything I didn't know already, but
somehow I heard a few details that tantalized me, like the fact that
T.S.Eliot was a chain-smoker and at various times in his life a very hard
drinker. And then we had a run-through quite near the end, which was a
disaster, from my point of view—everyone else was quite good. Then
something else happened: Max Stafford-Clark invited his father to talk to
us. He is called David Stafford-Clark and he is a leading psychiatric
theorists. Max had given him the play to read it as a case history. From the
play he was able to identify Eliot's symptoms or condition, and he
described *Tom and Viv* in psychiatric terms. Then we were able to quiz
him. The obvious question is: how did these people behave. He then said
that T.S.Eliot, from what you can gather from the play, hated life. And
David Stafford-Clark cited an incident he had come across: a person of
this type, every time he had a bath he would clean the bath tub, eight or
nine times, meticulously, after he had finished it. And when asked why he
said: "Well, I don't want any semen that might have come off me,
impregnate the next person, a woman, who might have a bath next". He
was told that semen dies within seconds. He said: "I know, but I still
cannot help myself". So that gave me a clue that T.S.Eliot was holding
himself in, keeping himself buttoned up. Most of what he did in his life
was trying to put real experience at some remove. Even his spiritual
experience was not done in a Shelleyan or Wordsworthian "me and

nature" way—it had to be mediated through the Church and the very orthodox and ritualised High Church at that. It was as if he was putting the whole world at one remove because he was afraid of it and hated it. This meeting with David gave me a clue for Eliot's contained mode of behaviour.

DMD
This explains the way you portrayed Eliot, as opposed to Mr. Hermann who probably did not have this approach. This attitude towards the part made the play more real, not so black and white

TW
I had to develop a performance that was suggestive, because it wasn't there, you never had a chance to explain it, so you had to be eminently suggestive. It was purely an actor's problem and generally the solution to that is to be enigmatic or to do as little as possible in order that you excite the imagination of the audience. You knew that they were going to be interested in T.S.Eliot. It wasn't as if you had come on stage and explain who you were; they would provide you with qualities that the play wasn't going to give you.

DMD
Did you have any chance to discuss there problems with Michael Hastings? Did he give any reasons why he did not show more of Eliot's genius?

TW
He did not. I wanted him to, and, had I done it again, in New York, I would have insisted that he showed something of Eliot's wit because he was a very witty man. He is rather an enigmatic writer, Michael Hastings, he writes rather instinctively: when you ask him the meaning of a line he would say: "I don't know what that means", which is not a great help. I think he is shy at the idea of writing about a genius being a genius, because Michael Hastings is a very talented man and not a genius, and T.S.Eliot clearly was. There is a problem.

DMD
What do you think is the message of *Tom and Viv*, if there is any?

TW

I was never convinced that it was a very good play and I think it is a very limited play. I mean I was very proud of it when we did it because it was very well acted. It was done as well as it possibly could be. It is very rarely when you do a play and you think: "Oh, this is as good as it can get, this production cannot get better, really". I did feel that about the first one. Chekhov it isn't, and I don't think it has any reverberations beyond an intriguing theatrical experience. In reading it I don't think you can get any real buzz.

DMD

Please comment on the relation of fact and fiction in *Tom and Viv* as discussed during rehearsals.

TW

There was an abiding problem for me and Max pertaining to the fact that we didn't feel that that was a true representation of T.S.Eliot. That was the basic frustration that we had. In many instances we felt that Eliot he couldn't have said that, and if he had said that he wouldn't have said it in that way. He was not an inarticulate person: T.S.Eliot spoke in sentences, in paragraphs, and if he was interrupted he would stop at the interruption and then carry on. If he was stopped in the middle of a sentence by "Oh Tom, you cannot mean that..." he would listen and then pick up the sentence exactly at the point where he had left it off, and then carry on and finish it. But Michael Hastings doesn't write in sentences. So there was that problem. You are much happier with Viv, really, because she could be anything, no one knows anything about her.

DMD

What did you think of the reviews of *Tom and Viv*?

TW

In so far as most of them were favourable towards the play and towards me personally, I was pleased with them. Actors usually have an ambiguous attitude towards critics. They are mostly wrong about everything they see. It is a curious relationship. There are two or three critics who do have a serious interest in the theatre. Most of them are craven, vulgar people, and it is best to keep out of their way, but unfortunately they do act as a censor of your professional life. You've read good reviews and you go along and seem the shows and you think: how can anybody think this is worth tuppence.

DMD

In your opinion, what part does suffering play in the artist's life? Is it a prerequisite to good quality in the artist's creation?

TW

That is an interesting one. It is a very right-wing view. That is what is behind the furore in this country about the Arts Council; artists should suffer, their work should be on the open market and should stand or fall by how popular it is. Keep them poor, that is the best thing. Look at Mozart: there is that view which is a very popular view about artists; it is certainly true that the massively subsidized theatres like the National do breed an incredible amount of complacency. Having worked at both institutions I know that to be the case. There are people there who, if for seconds they were scratching around freelance they wouldn't ever work again. But to return to your question whether artists should suffer—I mean there is financial suffering and spiritual suffering. Take for example Tolstoi. He was certainly not strapped to the toe, was he, he was a very rich man, and yet at the same time he suffered most of his life and was unhappy.

DMD

Is it because artists react more strongly to their environment, because they have a greater sensitivity?

TW

No, I don't think so. There are an equal number of artists who were contented throughout their lives. I was thinking of Oliver Goldsmith[9]. He was a very happy and affable, easy-going fellow, and there are a lot of people like that. I don't think Chekhov, although he was a very ill man, was a manifestly unhappy person. It is an image of the artist which was fostered by the romantic movement.

DMD

Do you think that "bio-plays" about artists are an attempt of the dramatist to come to terms with being an artist him/herself by experiencing what it was for someone else to have been an artist?

TW

It depends on the nature of the writer's preoccupations. Very often they write rather vulgar plays about artists which are simply trading on the name of the artist. I mean we were guaranteed interest in *Tom and Viv* because it was about T.S.Eliot and no one had written a play about

T.S.Eliot. You have to find someone nobody has ever written about and then you are going to generate some interest in that way. I think probably what people do is they use artists as a fulcrum, or a justification; they say: "Look, I feel this way about human relationships, I feel this way about politics, and so did Keats, or Shelley, they felt this way".

DMD
Emotions generally dominate the life of the artist; at least in biographical plays. Is that a cliché or fact?

TW
English theatre distrusts the intellect. The British on the whole like their artists to be rather like the popular image of Oscar Wilde. I remember seeing a film which portrayed him as a man of fun, and having a good time. They rather like their artists to be sportsmen who pen a couple of odes effortlessly, or a play and then go on to a party and then play cricket for England. They like that. They are very sentimental about artists, and I don't think this country has ever taken its artists very seriously. Peter Ustinov said that in the Soviet Union they pay the authors a compliment by putting them in jail, because they take them too seriously. But here, there is a long tradition to consider the artists as lovable eccentrics. So probably you will not get plays where people talk about ideas.

DMD
What about Stoppard[10]?

TW
In a sense, yes. He likes to dazzle his audience. It is a way of attracting attention to himself, people go out saying: "Jesus, Tom, you're really clever".

DMD
Among those plays, a large number are "one-person-shows" or two-handers. Do you think this is only because of financial/commercial reasons?

TW
It is incredibly easier to write one person and two person shows, much more easy than to write a show with seven or twenty people. I can see why they get done a lot, one-man shows about this and the other person; simply because actors spend a lot of time out of work and it is nice to have a little

project, Also how it is, you read somebody, become enthused by them and you want somehow to communicate your interest in these people. And money, of course, plays a great part.

Notes

1 Tom Wilkinson was born on December 12, 1948, in Leeds, West Yorkshire, England in a long line of urban farmers. Economic hardships had forced his family to move to Canada for a few years when he was a child. After he had returned to England, Wilkinson attended and graduated from the University of Kent at Canterbury with a degree in English and American Literature. before enrolling at the Royal Academy of Dramatic Art in the early 1970s. Within days of his graduation, he was lucky enough to land his first professional work with a company in Camden. By the 80s, the actor had joined the Royal Shakespeare Company and was singled out for his supporting work in a 1981 production of *Hamlet*. Wilkinson starred opposite Vanessa Redgrave in an acclaimed revival of Ibsen's *Ghosts*. Wilkinson first became active in film and television in the mid-1970s, specializing in playing men suffering from some emotional repression and/or pretensions of societal grandeur. He first became familiar to an international audience in 1997 with his role as one of six unemployed workers who strip for cash in 'Peter Catteneo's enormously successful and multiple Oscar-nominated comedy (including Best Picture) *The Full Monty* (1997). That same year, he was featured in Gillian Armstrong's *Oscar and Lucinda* (1997), and as the rabidly unpleasant father of Lord Alfred Douglas, Oscar Wilde's young lover in *Wilde* (1997). Wilkinson was also shown to memorable effect as a theatre financier with acting aspirations in the multiple Oscar-winning (including Best Picture) *Shakespeare in Love* (1998); also in 1998, he acted in one of his few leading roles in *The Governess* (1998), portraying a 19th century photographer with an eye for the film's title character (Minnie Driver). Wilkinson also developed a strong career on British television, returning to the stage occasionally, for example starring opposite Julia Ormond in *My Zinc Bed* by David Hare. Adapted from
http://www.hollywood.com/celebs/fulldetail/id/198204
http://www.tiscali.co.uk/entertainment/film/biographies/tom_wilkinson_biog.html
http://www.imdb.com/name/nm0929489/bio
2 T.S. Eliot (1888-1965), famous American-born poet, dramatist and essayist.
3 Michael Hastings (b. 1938) is a British dramatist and author of *Tom and Viv* about T.S. Eliot's first marriage to Vivienne Haigh-Wood.
4 Hastings, Michael. 1985. *Tom and Viv*. Harmondsworth: Penguin.
5 Herrmann, Edward (b. 1943) is an actor from the USA. He trained at the London Academy of Music and Dramatic Art (1968-9). He played Raymond Brock in David Hare's *Plenty* (1982), Siegfried Sassoon in Stephen MacDonald's *Not About Heroes* (1985), Richard Nelson's *The End of a Sentence*, and Rattigan's *The Deep Blue Sea* (1998, directed by Mark Lamos). Critics have commented on his ability to fade into the people he portrays. He is regularly cast in biographical roles also in

film and TV, having twice played Franklin Roosevelt. He also starred as baseball great Lou Gehrig. (Meyer-Dinkgräfe 2002, 121)

6 E[dward] P[almer] Thomson (1924-1993) was a British historian.

7 Max Stafford-Clark (b. 1941) was associate director at the Traverse Theatre Company in Edinburgh, and associate director, then artistic director at the Royal Court in London (1971-93). Since then he has run his own company, called *Out of Joint*, and is also a director in residence at the Royal Shakespeare Company. (Meyer-Dinkgräfe 2002, 287)

8 Peter Ackroyd (b. 1949), is a British author, writing both prose fiction and biographies.

9 Oliver Goldsmith (1730-1774), Irish writer, poet and dramatist.

10 Tom Stoppard (b. 1937), is a British dramatist. Important plays include *Rosencrantz and Guildenstern are Dead* (1966), *Jumpers* (1972), *Arcadia* (1993), *Indian Ink* (1994), and *The Invention of Love* (Royal National Theatre, 1997). Stoppard is a dramatist who is able to successfully merge highly sophisticated subject—matter and entertainment. (Abbreviated from (Meyer-Dinkgräfe 2002, 290)

Chapter Ten

Gertrude Stein and a Companion: Miriam Margolyes

Miriam Margolyes[1], who played Gertrude Stein[2] in *Gertrude Stein and a Companion*[3] by Win Wells, in a letter to DMD, 15.4.1985

DMD
During the last few years, the number of plays about poets, composers, actors, etc. (in short, artists) has increased considerably. Could you think of an explanation for this remarkable development

MM
I think that possibly the increase recently in bio-pic plays and films is as a result of the current "personality cults" which have been developed in recent years. The instance on the private life of famous people living today inevitably paralleled by an interest in dead-figures and as the more salacious aspects of their lives become public, it is felt that they are an easier target to portray on film and television and in the theatre, as they cannot answer back.

DMD
Among those plays, a large number are "one-person-shows" or two-handers. Do you think this is only because of financial/commercial reasons?

MM
Yes, I believe that the large number of one-woman shows or two-handers is solely because of financial/commercial restraints.

DMD
What is the function of a "bio-play"? Does it intend to give an insight into the life of a famous artist, or to convey a more universal message?

MM

I don't think there is a specific function of a "Bio-play" on an artist; it depends entirely on each play and each author's perception of his or her subject. Ideally, I think it should convey an insight into the life of a famous artist and can sometimes throw light onto hitherto inexplicable facets of that artist's work. The more universal message which you mention is the function of art generally, but one can only reach it by emphasis on the particular.

DMD

In your opinion, what part does suffering play in the artist's life? Is it a prerequisite to good quality in the artist's creation?

MM

I do not think that suffering is a prerequisite to good quality in the artists' creations. Suffering plays some part in life as any other part in life and I can only answer that "It all depends".

DMD

Do you think that "bio-plays" about artists are an attempt of the dramatist to come to terms with being an artist him/herself by experiencing what it was for someone else to have been an artist?

MM

Yes, in some cases.

DMD

How did you prepare for the portrayal of Gertrude Stein?

MM

I prepared for the part of Gertrude Stein by reading biographies and autobiographies, looking at photographs, reading her works and most usefully by listening to a tape of her voice. I did not actually try to reproduce her voice on stage, because it was a very mannered delivery which I felt would not be theatrically acceptable, but the timbre of her voice and certain inflections, I found very useful, also the slowness, repetitiveness of her inflection.

DMD

How would you describe the character as you portrayed her?

MM

To describe a character either living or dead is a difficult task but I will try. Gertrude Stein was primarily a magnificent egoist; she was physically large but handsome and vain of her appearance. Friends note that she used to caress her sculptured head as if enjoying the shape and feel of it. She was a jolly woman, who enjoyed social contact and laughter. She was generous and brave but extremely critical. Her homosexuality was probably total, but I believe that she enjoyed being lionized by both sexes, if not exactly sleeping with them. She believed deeply seriously in the craft of her writing and also that she was a world genius on the level of Picasso. In this later estimation, I believe she was mistaken and overestimated her powers. I have tried to be as accurate as possible in my presentation of Gertrude Stein, as I feel it is the actor's duty to reproduce the character as closely as possible to what is described by those who knew the character.

DMD

Have you found any particular difficulties in playing Gertrude Stein, and if so, how did you master them?

MM

The difficulties of playing Gertrude Stein are the same as playing any part but of course it is more difficult when playing the part of someone whom a lot of people have a preconceived notion of. She was American and so I had to master, not only the peculiarly deep tones of her voice but also her rather cultured American accent. She spoke and moved slowly and deliberately and I had to be careful not to get pompous and boring and therefore variation in pace is quite important. I mastered the difficulties simply by practice and getting more confidence in working on the text and very slowly feeling my way into the skin of the woman. It is a very common way of working.

Notes

1 Miriam Margolyes OBE studied English Literature at Cambridge University with Dr. FR Leavis. On leaving university, she joined the BBC Radio Drama Repertory Company & for a year played everything from little boys to old ladies. That started her love of voice work, which has resulted in a distinguished career recording books & animation features (she was Babe's mother Fly). Her recording of *The Queen and I*, in which she plays every member of the British Royal Family is the biggest-selling audio book in the world. She recently recorded the best-sellers, *Stuffed and Trody* for Harper Collins & won the Audie award for *Edith's Book* and

won the SWPA Best Recording for *Oliver Twist*. Since moving to the USA in 1989, she has made many films, including *Cold Comfort Farm*, *Little Dorrit* (which garnered her a Best Supporting Actress from the LA Critics Circle), *End of Days*, *Little Shop of Horrors*. She was the Nurse in Baz Lurhman's *Romeo and Juliet*, she won a BAFTA Best Supporting Actress Award for *The Age of Innocence* (directed by Martin Scorsese) and is Professor Sprout in *Harry Potter and the Chamber of Secrets*. Her West End theatre credits include *The Threepenny Opera* and *Orpheus Descending* (both with Vanessa Redgrave), *Kenndy's Children*, *The White Devil*, *She Stoops to Conquer* (for Sir Peter Hall) and *The Killing of Sister George*. She snatched a week from *Vagina Monologues* to perform *Dickens' Women* in New York and has just completed a sell-out season in *The Way of the World* for the Sydney Theatre Company. *Dickens' Women* has played to audiences in London's West End, where it won an Olivier nomination for Best Entertainment. Since its first showing at the Edinburgh Festival, it has been seen in Australia at the Sydney Festival, in India, South Africa & Israel. In Los Angeles, it was presented by Norman Lear & LA Theatreworks at the Tiffany Theatre. In 2002, Miriam was awarded an O.B.E. from HM The Queen for her services to Drama. (Adapted from
http://www.miriammargolyes.com/biography.php)
2 Gertrude Stein (1874-1946), American writer.
3 Wells, Win. *Gertrude Stein and a Companion*. Playscript 1621.

Chapter Eleven

Directing Byron, Shelley and Brenton: Roland Rees

Roland Rees[1] directed Howard Brenton's[2] *Bloody Poetry*. Interview with DMD, 21.3.1985.

DMD
During the last few years, the number of plays about poets, composers, actors, etc. (in short, artists) has increased considerably. Could you think of an explanation for this remarkable development

RR
There are more plays altogether, thus the number of bio-plays has also increased.

DMD
Among those plays, a large number are "one-person-shows" or two-handers. Do you think this is only because of financial/commercial reasons?

RR
There are no other reasons than commercial ones.

DMD
In your opinion, what part does suffering play in the artist's life? Is it a prerequisite to good quality in the artist's creation?

RR
It is not a necessity, but a good work is hardly being written without the author having had experience—suffering.

DMD
What do you think is the artist's relation to love, sex (emotions in general)?

RR
From my experience with writers, they are indeed highly emotional people.

DMD
Do you think that "bio-plays" about artists are an attempt of the dramatist to come to terms with being an artist him/herself by experiencing what it was for someone else to have been an artist?

RR
In Howard Brenton's case, definitely. He has aspects of both Byron and Shelley. He loves talking to enthusiastic listeners, with a bottle of good wine, for hours. On the other hand he has those qualities of Shelley, being passionate, romantic and all that. This is on a personal level. Otherwise, Shelley's problem is that he was not subsidized, and his work was never published within his lifetime (He did not know that there were secret editions). Howard knows that that might be where he would be without subsidy, however sparingly it is being distributed. I commissioned the play from Howard, and he was very interested from the beginning. We conceived the play in an epic structure, with many characters. After his return form the USA (for the opening of *Genius*), Howard had completely changed his approach towards the family aspects of Shelley and Byron. He was present during rehearsals and did a little rewriting when necessary.

Notes

1 Roland Rees co-founder as Artistic Director Foco Novo, one of the earliest, innovative touring UK Fringe Theatre companies. He commissioned and directed many new plays, including 'The Elephant Man', seen in his Foco Novo production at the Hampstead Theatre and the National Theatre. The play went to Broadway, and the story was later filmed. (From the website of *Oberon books*, http://www.oberonbooks.com)
2 Howard Brenton (b. 1942) is associated with socialist writing at the Royal Court theatre in London. In 1969, his play *Revenge* was produced at the Royal Court Upstairs, and toured by David Hare's company Portable Theatre. The Royal Court also presented Brenton's *Magnificence* (1973). *Bloody Poetry* (1984) deals with poets Byron and Shelley, *Pravda*, (National Theatre, 1985), about contemporary newspaper politics, starred Anthony Hopkins and proved a popular success. (Meyer-Dinkgräfe 2002, 38).

CHAPTER TWELVE

THE WORDS OF THE CRITIC:
IRVING WARDLE

Irving Wardle[1], theatre critic of *The Times*, Interview with DMD,
27.2.1985

DMD
During the last few years, the number of plays about poets, composers,
actors, etc. (in short, artists) has increased considerably. Could you think
of an explanation for this remarkable development

IW
From the 50s onwards, dramatists put their emphasis on subjects of direct
experience rather than subjects from books. Maybe after 25 years of that,
there is enough of it. Playwrights do no longer want to write "end-of-
Britain" plays; Brenton[2], for example. Moreover, biographical plays before
that could be rather bad, the lines great poets had to speak. There are more
creative writers today, better dramatists.

DMD
Among those plays, a large number are "one-person-shows" or two-
handers. Do you think this is only because of financial/commercial
reasons?

IW
There is no other reason.

DMD
What is the function of a "bio-play"? Does it intend to give an insight into
the life of a famous artist, or to convey a more universal message?

IW
To get under the skin of the audience. To show the private life of a famous person, the discrepancy between a great poet and his ordinary private day-to-day life.

DMD
In your opinion, what part does suffering play in the artist's life? Is it a prerequisite to good quality in the artist's creation?

IW
This idea is from the romantic tradition.

DMD
Do you think that "bio-plays" about artists are an attempt of the dramatist to come to terms with being an artist him/herself by experiencing what it was for someone else to have been an artist?

IW
The dramatist should already have an idea of what it is like to be an artist, because he has written plays before.

Notes

1 Irwing Wardle worked as an editor and theatre critic for *The Times Educational Supplement* (1956-9), *the Observer* (1959-63), *The Times* (1963-1989) and *The Independent*. He wrote two books, *The Theatre of George Devine* (Jonathan Cape, 1976) and *Theatre Criticism* (Routledge, 1992).
2 Howard Brenton (b. 1942) is associated with socialist writing at the Royal Court theatre in London. See interview with Roland Rees in chapter eleven of this book, who directed Brenton's *Bloody Poetry*.

PART II:

BOULEVARD COMEDY IN GERMANY

CHAPTER THIRTEEN

SIXTY YEARS IN THE THEATRE:
ALFONS HÖCKMANN

Alfons Höckmann[1], founder and artistic director of the Komödie Düsseldorf, Germany (1968-2003), in interview with DMD on 9 April 2001.

AH
A turbulent afternoon

DMD
I can well imagine that.

AH
Because we had the phone call [announcing that the lead actress of the current production was ill and had to withdraw from the performance] at around 11 am, and then I had to arrange for her replacement. She [Ulla Martens] solved that very well, didn't she?

DMD
Yes, indeed, and the audience was very appreciative as well. They appreciate the achievement of an actress taking over at such short notice.

AH
If we had had to cancel the performance it would have been disastrous for us. But she has many years of experience of course.

DMD
And she has appeared at the Komödie many times before.

AH
Yes, over the last few years, more and more. She replaced Ingrid[2] several times. Also in the play we are rehearsing now, *Barfuß in Park*[3], she plays the part that Ingrid should have been playing. But she is very, very ill. She has been in hospital for the past three weeks, and no end in sight. You have had an interesting few days now?

DMD
Yes, Ayckbourn's *Raucher/Nichtraucher* [*Intimate Exchanges*] in Berlin, with Katja Riemann[4] and Erik Uwe Laufenberg[5], who also directed. Magnier's *Oscar* in Dresden, with local stars, Patricia Levrey's *Herz und Beinbruch* (*Break a Leg*) in Munich, Kleine Komödie am Max II, with Grit Böttcher[6] and Thomas Reiner[7].

AH
What was that like?

DMD
She did not remain in character enough, and I don't understand why in a French play she pronounces her husband's name like the German "Michel"—it should be Michèl.

AH
At least if it is still set in France. If you transport it to Germany, you can use the German pronunciation

DMD
But then all the other names should be rendered in German as well, which they were not, so it was inconsistent. Then I saw Karin Beier's[8] production of *Affaire Rue Lurcine*, by Labiche, in Cologne, at the municipal theatre.

AH
What was that like?

DMD
Just as you would expect a municipal theatre to do a comedy. Whatever is typical of boulevard comedy was just not there. And many things were added, to make the interpretation of the text stronger.

AH
Yes, added from the outside. To make it interesting—just look at all the things I thought of.

DMD
For example, one of the characters looks into the funnel of an old record player, and a cloud of soot comes out, making his face all black. I can't imagine that was in the original text of the play…

AH
The worst thing I saw of Beier was *Romeo and Juliet*, some five or six years ago at the Schauspielhaus, here. She had the balcony scene on two swings. Romeo and Juliet are sitting on swings, quite high up, swinging next to each other. How can any atmosphere develop, like that, an atmosphere of the night, when he must not be too loud, so as not to be heard by the enemies. No atmosphere can develop at all, like that.

> [O, speak again, bright angel! for thou art
> As glorious to this night, being o'er my head
> As is a winged messenger of heaven
> Unto the white-upturned wondering eyes
> Of mortals that fall back to gaze on him
> When he bestrides the lazy-pacing clouds
> And sails upon the bosom of the air.] Act II scene 2

You cannot say that, swinging. In such moments I think of Leopold Lindtberg[9] in Zurich. He said that during lyrical passages, no-one was allowed to move. When other characters were also on stage, one movement, he said, could destroy the entire atmosphere.

DMD
And yesterday Theater an der Kö.

AH
Diderot[10]. The main actor[11] was too physical for my taste, not spiritual enough, the atmosphere he spreads, and as a result… he just is not right for the part, also because of his thinning hair. Has played a detective on TV, he was good for that. I saw that production last week. The wife was good

DMD
But only in the play for the 1ˢᵗ Act, then the author just dropped her.

AH

And the main actress is not bad, but she lacked brio. And the play you saw yesterday, [Gunter Phillip[12], *Da Wird Daddy Staunen*], it's a bit long. It could be about a quarter of an hour shorter. And the main attraction is of course this comedian[13].

DMD

Yes, it's amazing the way he controls his body.

AH

Yes, it's full command of the body. And it does not come across as artificial, because it all comes from his cranky personality. This is the secret of all comical parts. Just as you said about the French play you saw in Munich…

DMD

Break a Leg [*A cloche pied,* by Patricia Levrey], with Grit Boettcher

AH

Grit Boettcher, again, is one of those actresses who approaches the comedy from outside. Flat. Whereas this comedian, it's pure poetry.

DMD

What would you say is special about directing boulevard comedy?

AH

It's something that Leopold Lindtberg said. Lindtberg worked with the Stadttheater in Düsseldorf before he went to Zürich in 1932. Then he was the first director with Leonard Steckel at the Schauspielhaus Zurich. And then he directed a lot at the Burgtheater in Vienna. And he briefly was with Gründgens[14], where he directed *Hamlet*. He said: "The best director is the one you don't notice". I am proud that my audiences often tell me that they hardly have the feeling that they are watching theatre. And that is the opposite of what you said about the Labiche production, there they did do theatre, as it is done in a municipal theatre. The metier of boulevard is much more difficult than serious theatre as far as its craft is concerned. Because there the plot, often the tragedy, carries the weight. But in boulevard, here, for example, in Gunter Phillip's play, there is also a message, birth control, but the emphasis is on the aperçus, the fun, that Phillip uses to keep the audience entertained. My concern is articulation, which I placed much emphasis on right from the beginning of my career, already in training. This training means that I can speak long sentences without taking breath, or without anyone noticing that, while I am speaking, I am taking a deep breath. The audience must not hear this.

DMD
You have recently added special programmes to the repertory of the *Komödie Düsseldorf*. Why?

AH
Yes, we did not do that in earlier years. We only started this three years ago. It really started with Günter Stratmann, Doctor Stratmann, who rented a house from the town of Essen to do his shows. He was active as a GP in nearby Bottrop, and did cabaret while he was a student. His show became more and more popular. He chats, in a slight local accent, and makes fun of the situations he encounters as a GP. His programmes usually sell out completely.

DMD
And I saw a poster for a Zarah Leander[15] evening

AH
Yes. That Zarah Leander evening. This singer is an exciting discovery. This woman comes from Sweden and is great, a woman who is really able to revive Zarah Leander. Also because her voice is so close to Zarah Leander, when you hear her singing the chansons. That also is part of the additional Monday evening program, which actually goes against the comedy repertory.

DMD
In that context, I wanted to ask you how you see your position here in Düsseldorf, especially since the Theater an der Kö opened a few years ago.

AH
Yes, that is a chapter that is not so nice. That a family with whom we were friends suddenly opens a second boulevard theatre. We had not heard anything about it. The building was formerly the home of the Rheinische Post[16]. When they moved out, the building became available. The same architect who created the Kö-Galerie, also built the Schadow-Arkaden. And because people don't really much go to those areas of the city, they thought if they put a theatre there… Anyway, it is of course more difficult for two theatres. That is quite obvious. Not more difficult as far as selling

tickets on the open market is concerned, but selling through the theatre organisations. What they can sell to their subscribers is now halved in the area of boulevard theatre. In addition there is now the Kapitol theatre with its musicals, which provides further competition. We were forced, as a result, to raise our season from four to five productions. Simply because the potential of spectators whom we need to fill the theatre at the beginning of the week is only half as strong as before. In addition, these theatre organisations themselves have suffered a reduction of members, because today's generation of theatre goers does not like to be restricted by subscription—they want to decide ad hoc. That's just a fact you have to come to terms with. The old subscription system we know from our parents and which the children inherited, is a phase-out model. It can only get more difficult. The opera house and the Schauspielhaus notice that as well. Especially the Schauspielhaus. Once they notice it, they tamper with the number of rows of seats. Take out two rows, enlarge the proscenium.

DMD
Is that now also a criterion for selecting plays for the season?

AH
Yes, this young colleague, Robby Heinersdorff[17], has the ambition to present problem plays. Like the Diderot that you saw. And you saw how many came. What was it like? When did you see it?

DMD
On Sunday for the earlier, 6pm performance. I would say 90%

AH
That many? I am surprised. When I saw it, on the Friday before that, it was only a third! 90% is a very good evening. But you will have seen that seats are missing on the sides.

DMD
Yes, indeed. Perhaps because of the sight lines?

AH
No, that is merely for psychological reasons. Because you can see very well from those sides. The auditorium was originally for 450 seats, which is a little more than we have, but as it is arranged now, there's space for only 350. And we notice that the people who come to us say that they just want to laugh. We did try to include problem plays. There is an American

play, set in an old people's home, where son in law and daughter in law visit once a month, and the father says: Sunday again...! And you can notice that they are a bit bored there. A very good play. The people then say, oh, yes, an interesting play, but I've got a nursing case at home as well. Those are plays that deal with human needs and worries... But the play by Gunter Phillip

DMD
Yes, I listened to what people said to each other during the interval, and even after the performance on the underground people were still talking about Ganser, commenting on the way he moves, still with a smile on their faces.

AH
And this is how we create our seasons. Anything else would be pointless. For example, to say that I want to play some classical roles again, which I have played anyway, 90% of them. I have developed a very nice alternative here, with evenings where I read texts, poetry. For example, last Sunday in the Goethe museum, I read from Goethe's *West-östliche Diwan*, and 120 people came and reacted very positively. It is at such occasions that I can fully live out my classical training in speaking. It was the forth event of this kind.

Notes

1 Alfons Höckmann was born in 1923, the fifth of eleven children, in Dortmund. His father owned a bakery. Höckmann, like his future wife Braut, never wanted to pursue a different career than that of an actor. He took acting classes and in 1941, while still attending Gymnasium he was successful in his second attempt to gain admission to what was then leading drama school in Germany, the Westfälische Schauspielschule in Bochum. Its director, Saladin Schmitt accepted him as the last student before the school had to close, later in 1941, because of the war. Höckmann soon became a member of the theatre company in Bochum, which was led by Schmitt. He was recruited and spent the years of 1943-45 with the navy in Tuscany. After the war, Höckmann returned to the company in Bochum. Further stages in his career were at the theatres in Baden-Baden, Munich, Lübeck, Nuremberg, Zurich, and Schauspielhaus in Düsseldorf. In 1968, the Steinstrasse theatre building in Düsseldorf was available; Höckmann had become less satisfied with his work at the Schauspielhaus and his wife, actress and soprano Ingrid Braut, too, was ready for independence. They founded the Komödie-Boulevardtheater Düsseldorf. (Meyer-Dinkgräfe 2005, 19-22)

2 Ingrid Braut (1926-2001) was Höckmann's wife and co-founder of the Komödie Düsseldorf. Her father was a merchant, her mother a secretary. From her father she

inherited her desire to remain independent; her mother played the piano (her grandfather was a piano maker with Steinway&Sons) and Braut learned playing at the age of five. Early on she developed the desire to become an actress, taking up acting and singing lessons as well as ballet classes while still at school. The arts were also represented on her father's side of the family: one uncle was film-star Hans-Hermann Schaufuß. (Meyer-Dinkgräfe 2005, 19-22)

3 The hit play by Neil Simon.

4 Katja Riemann (b. 1963), German actress, predominantly on TV and film.

5 Eric Uwe Lauffenberg (b. 1960), German actor, director and artistic director.

6 Grit Böttcher (b. 1938), German actress who performed on stage mainly in the boulevard comedy genre, in addition to a TV and film career.

7 Thomas Reiner was born and grew up in Stuttgart. He began his training as an actor while still attending secondary school. Early employments were with the theatres in Esslingen, Stuttgart, Bremen, Heidelberg, Kassel, Baden-Baden and Bochum. In 1956 he moved to Munich and has worked there on a freelance basis since, in theatre, TV, film and dubbing.

8 Karin Beier (b. 1966) While studying Drama and English at Köln University, Beier founded a Shakespeare company and directed nine of Shakespeare's plays in various locations inspired by the plays, such as churches, castle gardens and factories. The managing director of the theatre in Düsseldorf saw one of these productions and invited her to work as an assistant director at his theatre, later to proceed to her own independent work. In 1993 her production of *Romeo and Juliet* opened the theatre season of the Schauspielhaus in Düsseldorf, and since then she has directed there regularly, as well as in Hamburg and Bonn. Company work has been described as her strength: with an international group of actors from nine European countries she presented *A Midsummer Night's Dream* (1995), and plans further international collaborations. More recent productions include Ionesco's *The Chairs*, Düsseldorf, 1996, *Twelfth Night* (Hamburg, 1996), and Measure for Measure (Hamburg, 1998). From 2007 she will serve as artistic director of the Cologne municipal theatre. (Meyer-Dinkgräfe 2002, 25).

9 Leopold Lindtberg (1902-1984). Born in Vienna, he worked at theatres in Germany in the 1920s. In the early 1930s he emigrated to Paris. In 1933 he joined the theatre in Zurich, Switzerland; later he turned to film.

10 French writer Denis Diderot (1713-1984) is the main character in Eric Emmanuel Schmitt's play *Le Libertin* (Der Freigeist / The Free Spirit).

11 The part of Diderot was played by Wold-Dietrich Berg. Born in Danzig, he grew up in the Ruhr-area of Germany and trained as an actor in Bochum. Early work was with the theatres in Essen and Dortmund. In 1972 he joined the company of the Deutsches Schauspielhaus in Hamburg. For many years he worked in film and television, gaining particular popularity as a detective in a well-known crime series, *Tatort*.

12 Gunter Phillip (1918-2004) trained as an actor at the Max Reinhardt Seminar, Vienna. He also studied medicine and became a consultant specialist neurologist, practicing in Vienna for more than seven years. In 1949 he turned to his artistic career, writing more than 100 features for radio, thirteen programs for cabaret,

twenty-one film scripts and three boulevard comedies. He starred in more than 150 films.

13 Marcus Ganser played the part of Dr Berny Bedford in Phillip's *Da wird Daddy Staunen*. He is a multi-talented artist, combining work as an actor, scene designer, director in theatre and radio, and radio editor and presenter .

14 German actor, director and artistic director Gustaf Gründgens (1899-1963)

15 Swedish actress and singer, 1907-1981, who was particularly successful in Germany.

16 Name of the largest regional newspaper in the Düsseldorf area.

17 René Heinersdorff, member of the artistic management of the Theater am Dom, Cologne and until 2003 of the Kleines Theater am Max II in Munich and sole artistic manager of the Theater an der Kö in Düsseldorf, was born in 1963 and thus belongs to the younger generation of boulevard comedy theatre artistic directors. After his Abitur, he studied German and Philosophy at the University in Düsseldorf and received his training as an actor and director from Harald Leipnitz (1926-2000), a respected film and television actor who, later in his career, turned increasingly to acting in and directing boulevard comedy. Heinersdorff also took singing lessons with Ruth Grünhagen, a renowned Düsseldorf-based teacher. He appeared at theatres in Berlin, Hamburg, Munich, Cologne, Düsseldorf, where he directed more than forty productions. In addition he was very active on television, not only in parts in individual episodes, but also in ongoing parts for long-running series and as a director (http://www.theatreanderkoe.de/). (Meyer-Dinkgräfe 2005, 23)

CHAPTER FOURTEEN

TWO THEATRES, ACTING AND DIRECTING: CLAUS HELMER

Claus Helmer[1], artistic director of the Komödie and the Fritz Rémond Theater im Zoo, in Frankfurt/Main, in interview with DMD, 27.10.2003

DMD
You have now run this house [Komödie] since 1972

CH
Yes, since 1972. Where we are now is the fourth building. Herr Kolleg, my predecessor, founded the theatre at the Roßmarkt, in 1950. He was there for two years, but because the building was a ruin, he had to vacate. Then he opened the Theater am Roßmarkt number two. Then in 1962 he opened the Komödie, close to here, and I took that over in 1972, with a lot of debt. In 1998 the entire building was torn down. It took a lot of negotiating to get the current Komödie integrated into this new house. We presented our own drawings, and they accepted them, and we opened the new stage in 1999.

DMD
And you also run the Fritz Rémond Theater im Zoo.

CH
Yes, I took that over nine years ago. Also a kind of cloak and dagger operation. The city asked me to take over because my predecessor had left debts of 2.3 million DM. Not so easy, it cost me many sleepless nights. I had played for Rémond[2] a lot, and I felt that it was my duty to maintain what he had created, now that he did not live any more. In a short period of time I had reduced the debts by 1.5 million, and the city abated the remaining DM 800,000.

DMD
How do you manage to combine your roles as artistic director and manager of two theatres, with directing and acting?

CH
You know, it just developed like that. I have to make sure that I get both houses full, because financially we depend to 70% on sold seats. I went to the theatre as an actor, but I had to reduce that area and cannot perform as much as in earlier years. Every season I direct two productions and act in a third one. That makes already nine months. And in addition to that all the office work both here and at the Zoo theatre. I have to select the plays for both stages, have to cast and negotiate contracts. A lot to do… And times don't get better—times are more and more against the theatre: as a result of the recession, people save money; and those who say they don't notice are merely lying. London and Paris have the advantage of being centralised. In Germany there are so many more theatres closely together.

DMD
How does your audience here react to Ayckbourn?

CH
I was among those who took pains to develop an understanding for Ayckbourn, in some cases with first German productions, and all of them were very successful.

DMD
How interesting, because I have heard repeatedly that Ayckbourn is difficult for boulevard comedy theatre audiences.

CH
There are theatres that do only farces, and there it is more difficult with Ayckbourn, because he has always a different starting point. Here at the Komödie my seasons are not geared only towards farces. I also did a musical play about Marlene Dietrich. Or a musical such as *Irma la Douce*, or *Kiss Me Kate*. There are theatres where people go and if they can roar with laughter they had a good evening. I love farces, the English are so brilliant at them, Cooney[3] is one of my favourite authors, great. For me he is the Ionesco of boulevard theatre. So I try to mix the seasons. Comedy, farce, something with a tendency towards the serious, such as Ayckbourn. What makes it difficult is that only insiders know how difficult and serious boulevard theatre is. It has to be serious, otherwise it degenerates to a

series of clichés, get up, light a cigarette, drink a whiskey, sit down, get up—that is terrible. And that's why the reputation can be so bad, if they can't do it properly or if they do it as if it were easy, if they lack the appropriate seriousness in their approach.

DMD

Do you feel that German audiences are more critical as far as the plot of a comedy is concerned?

CH

Yes, you are right, in Germany you have to be more precise. I remember seeing a comedy in London, set in a hotel. In one scene there is a suitcase in the room on the left, and then in the next scene it was suddenly in the room on the right. Why? How does it get there? No problem in London. But here we are all so thorough. In Germany we just don't have much of a comedy tradition. *Minna von Barnhelm*[4], *Der Zerbrochene Krug*[5], *Der Biberpelz*[6], that's all. In Austria there is Nestroy, and Molière in France. The Germans have nothing much to offer. In more recent times there's Flatow[7], but that's really limited to two good entertainment value plays, *Das Geld liegt auf der Bank* and *Der Mann, der sich nicht traut....*

DMD
And nowadays Stephan Vögel[8].

CH
A highly talented chap, quite extraordinary for a German speaker, how to the point he writes. We can only hope that such writing is supported and stays.

Notes

1 Claus Helmer. From 1959 to 1962 he trained at the Max Reinhardt Seminar in Vienna. Between 1956 and 1960 he already appeared in forty parts on most Vienna stages, as well as in three film and numerous TV productions. His first contract in Germany was in Düsseldorf, 1962-64. From 1965, Helmer worked as freelance actor and director in Aachen, Düsseldorf, Hamburg, Stuttgart und Frankfürt am Main. In 1965 saw his debut at the Fritz Rémond theatre in Frankfurt, followed in 1967 with the debut at the Komödie in Frankfurt. Since 1972 he has been director of the Komödie. In 1995 he also took over the directorship of the Fritz Rémond theatre. He holds numerous public honours, including a professorial title from the federal president of Austria. Adapted from
http://www.diekomoedie.de/komoedie/ensemble/index.html

2 Fritz Rémond (1902-1976) was a German actor, director and artistic director, cousin of actor and playwright Curt Goetz. Until 1936, Rémond lived in Prague as an actor; in 1947, he founded the Kleines Theater im Zoo in Frankfurt/Main in a building that originally formed part of the Frankfurt Zoo. The suggestion to start that theatre came from the zoo's director, Bernard Grzimek.

3 Ray Cooney is one of the leading writers of farce in the UK today.

4 Comedy written in 1767 by Gotthold Ephraim Lessing (1729-1781)

5 Comedy written in 1811 by Heinrich von Kleist (1777-1811)

6 Comedy written in 1893 by Gerhart Hauptmann (1862-1946)

7 Curth Flatow (b 1920). He is the most well-known and popular representative of so-called boulevard comedy. Flatow has to date written more than twenty plays for this genre. Since 1950 he has also been active writing for film, radio and television.

8 Stefan Vögel (b. 1969), Austrian dramatist, representing the much-needed younger generation of comedy writers.

CHAPTER FIFTEEN

STARTING YOUR OWN THEATRE:
ANGELIKA OBER

Angelika Ober, actress and artistic director of the Boulevard Münster, in interview with DMD, 30 October 2003.

DMD
You founded the Boulevard Münster in 1997. Could you please tell me how this idea developed?

AO
When they appointed a new artistic manager for Münster's municipal theatre, they suggested to me to resign, so that the incoming manager did not have to keep me on, as I was tenured, as it were, he could not have sacked me, and they did not want to burden him with a performer he might not want to have on his team. So then I was faced with some decisions. I had been living in Münster for the past thirteen years, I had my home here and my partner, and so I thought that I really don't want to leave Münster. I could have joined the state theatre in Oldenburg. Their artistic director had directed some productions here in Münster and would have been interested for me to join him in Oldenburg. But I really wanted to stay here. And then I thought that over the last few years in Münster I had repeatedly thought of doing something on my own, because I had become fed up with finding out what parts I play from a list pinned to the notice board, and what parts other colleagues get, and how that matches with the parts I would have liked to play. And then to match up which colleague went on holidays with the director and got a good part, I was really fed up with all that, because I am not the kind of person to suck up to people. So all that had been going on in my mind already when the change-over of artistic manager came about. Today I am really grateful to the incoming manager because it is so different to be one's own master. The newspaper came to see me and wanted to interview me because I was considered an

audience favourite and had to leave, and I simply told them: "don't worry, I will open up my own theatre here in Münster". It was just an idea, at the time, which I just blurted out, and as soon as I had done so, people jumped at the idea. My family threw up their arms in horror, and then I really sat down with them, with my sister, who now does most of the sets, together with my partner, Peter Pittermann, and they all said: "If you really manage to pull this one off, it will be most impressive"! Yes, and then I started doing some calculations. I put together a season, I read plays, bought myself a computer. As a mere actress, so to speak, I didn't have one. Then I chose the kinds of plays that I immediately liked and decided to use them for the season design. Then I started contacting directors with whom I had worked in the past and whom I liked whether they wanted to be part of the project. After I had finished designing a full season, with plays and directors and cast and all, I went to the bank and asked them what the chances were for them to support me. In the meantime I had also looked around for a suitable venue. I had been in touch with Herr Görtz, who owns an attractive shopping arcade in the city centre. Down here, where the theatre is now, he had owned a disco, which had gone bankrupt, and he didn't have any good luck with this area at all. So when I first approached him he told me he could not offer the space to me because he had offered it to the people who run the shop that is above, as a store room. So I said to myself I have to continue looking. After two months he phoned me and asked me whether I was still interested. In the meantime I had become interested in a different venue, where I would have had to finance it all by myself, and the space was much smaller than this one. So he called me, as I said, the idea had stuck with him, and asked me whether I was still looking for a venue, and I said yes. Then we sat down together and I presented him with all the plays that I had selected for the first season, and the budget which I had developed with my sister and my partner. I had called other theatres to ask what they spend on salaries and so on, I had theatres send me program brochures, and had travelled around a lot to get ideas and information about subscription systems. And on that basis Herr Görtz said that he would like to get involved. That he would like to build a beautiful theatre here, that he would finance the building. I pay €5000 rent a month, only for the space. He invested three quarters of a million (DM), and he of course calculated that in due course he will get his investment back. I invested DM 250,000. All the features in this theatre are designer-made: the seats, for example, are from the UK. Peter Sieger was the designer. He is quite a famous designer, all very exquisite. So then I went to the bank and told them: "Herr Görtz pays for the design of the entire space, and I contribute the stage technology, lights etc.". I got the loan, probably because of Görtz's involvement, because otherwise it would have been an entire million, which is of course a lot to ask for. The bank took four months to decide. Once I had their OK, I started casting the first season. We started rehearsing and they started building. On 13 December 1997 the curtain rose here for the first time. All this from the spontaneous, angry decision to open up my own theatre. But it is really like this: if you really want something in life, if it's not something you really cannot possibly achieve, like flying to the moon, so if it's something you can achieve from within your own energies, then you can do it.

DMD
What is your general view of boulevard comedy in Germany?

AO
When I was still with the municipal theatre, I also went to see boulevard; and you can get very good boulevard and there is really bad boulevard. And sometimes I hear things, how totally irresponsibly some people behave, just giving their actors video cassettes and telling them: "have a look at that, that's how we want you to play this part". And that's when you start getting poor boulevard. Because boulevard is a special kind of theatre. It all depends very much on rhythm, you have to develop a feeling for that rhythm, and you have to take it on board. In most cases you can't just play the boulevard plays at sight. You have to be very imaginative as a director.

DMD
How long has this current production been running?

AO
Exactly one month now.

DMD
In your experience, does it change in the course of a run?

AO
It changes in so far as it gets easier. But some things begin to drag, something which I personally don't like. When I direct something and look at it some time later, there are some changes that I like very much, but in some cases I have to be alert and careful and I take them on board as well. When I see something, I immediately tell the actors where some fads have crept in, where they don't stick with the agreements any more. I

mean, it does not happen all that often, but when it does, I immediately say: "not like this". Because if you have directed something, then you have given it a specific track, and when has been directed well, it stays on track.

DMD
So that it does not suddenly collapse?

AO
Yes. When I direct, I usually start with the first act, then I go on, then I go back to the first act, and so on, first, second, first, second, third, first, second, third, forth, etc. There are directors who race through an entire play in two weeks, that's madness. That's just not good, and I always notice when directors have raced through the play, there the nuances are missing and it's the nuances you have to practice and practice and practice.

DMD
I am asking this because I saw a production of Vögel's[2] *Eine Gute Partie* in Düsseldorf in July, and then again, with the same cast, in Frankfurt now in October. And that production changed considerably over those three to four months.

AO
Yes, That's the difference. You can refine it and you have to know where to refine. We had a production here some time ago, there we also refined it over the run. The opening night, as a result, was not as good as the last performance. But as I said, it depends whether you have raced through the play during rehearsals. When I direct, I know that I have four weeks time. And I need to trust myself and prepare well. The insecure directors are those who don't trust themselves and their ideas: "let's see what I thought about", and they then say to the actors: "try this or that". That's no good. You have to have your own concept when you direct a production. And that's the kind of directors I work with here, those who are imaginative. I found that actors who are also directing are for me the better directors, because they approach the rehearsals differently; they are more patient and they know that actors sometimes need more time to allow the ideas to mature in themselves, so that they don't have to constantly think about what they are doing. Directors who also work as dramaturg, for example, expect that once they have developed an idea, it stays. And then they are surprised when it does not stay, when it's all gone again. But it is indeed

always gone again. When I learn my lines, I do that in the mornings, and I repeat what we did the day before. What I rehearsed today I repeat tomorrow. Then I have to remember what we did, and 80% of it will be gone. That's just how it is. That's somehow how the brain works. And an actor who is also a director knows all that from their own experience. And they understand it. But directors who are not an actors tend to get impatient, "goodness me, we have rehearsed this so often now, it should really work now". An actor would never say that.

DMD
Yes, quite frustrating. Our students are not doing an actor training course, but an academic one. It was a new experience for them to loose again and again what they thought they had developed, they tended to get frustrated and didn't understand why it happened.

AO
Yes, that's normal. You have to practice. All these nuances, the glances, for example this sneezing number in the production you just saw, I hope it's still as I directed it, I have to have another look at it;;; you just practice that very, very often. It has to be very precise.

DMD
Did you already develop a feeling for the kind of audiences in Münster through your thirteen years with the municipal theatre?

AO
In my case, I talked to the audiences a lot, and they often said: "We really would like to laugh, we want to relax, we don't always want to see everything grey in grey." Because it had become almost a habit at the municipal theatre to have grey sets and grey costumes, and the plays tended to become greyer as well.

DMD
Indeed? I was in Düsseldorf yesterday, at the Schauspielhaus, where I saw Labiche, *Affaire Rue de Lurcine*. I just had to laugh, because everything was grey there as well. I saw Karin Beier's[3] production of that play in Cologne a year and a half ago, all grey as well. I went there to see the difference, boulevard in a boulevard theatre and in a municipal theatre.

AO

Yes, that's exactly what it is like. There are some directors at municipal theatres who are excellent at directing comedy, and others direct the comedy away. Simply away. Anyway, the spectators said, "we want to laugh", and I knew then that there is a real niche here. And I always enjoyed playing comedy. Now of course the ordinary actor plays comedy and then looks forward to playing tragedy, or the other way round. At municipal theatres that's how it is, you play repertory, and that includes everything. But here you do only comedies. That's why I have a thriller in every season, which has this serious element in it. But when we did *Gaslight / Gaslicht*, I realised that people didn't much like it. They wanted to laugh. They found it too serious, although it was a very good production. I have to draw my conclusions from that: when I do thrillers, I will do thriller comedies, and the audiences want to see those. I think that perhaps in five years, when the theatre is further established here, maybe I can risk a straightforward thriller again, such as *The Mousetrap*. But until then only thriller comedies. So I really have to offer comedy here.

DMD

The theatre's relationship with the press is very good, I take it, no slating review yet?

AO

No, you are right, no roasting yet. The newspapers recognise that Münster has its own boulevard theatre, and a good one at that. I am proud to say that the boulevard theatre has become mainstream in Münster.

DMD

In many other places, boulevard theatre is more or less ignored by the newspapers…or they send the apprentices

AO

Yes, I know. Not here. They make an effort, they appreciate us. Great!

DMD

You work with a subscription scheme, in addition to conventional sales?

AO

Yes, I don't have any subsidies, anything at all, no sponsoring. Nobody, nothing. That's why I have to live from the seat prices. We have around 350 subscribers; I have the boulevard day, the cheap day, where a ticket costs €13, it's always well attended. Wednesday and Thursday are also cheaper, €16 or €18, and weekends are 18, 21, 24 and 26, depending, and there is a super subscription for Sundays, saving 20%, for the ordinary subscription they save 15%. I have a number of special offers, and they are all made use of.

DMD
Also for senior citizens?

AO
Yes, as well. 5pm on Saturdays always, also very, very well attended.

Notes

1 Curth Flatow (b 1920). He is the most well-known and popular representative of so-called boulevard comedy. Flatow has to date written more than twenty plays for this genre. Since 1950 he has also been active writing for film, radio and television.
2 Stefan Vögel (b. 1969), Austrian dramatist, representing the much-needed younger generation of comedy writers.
3 Karin Beier (b. 1966) While studying Drama and English at Köln University, Beier founded a Shakespeare company and directed nine of Shakespeare's plays in various locations inspired by the plays such as churches, castle gardens and factories. The managing director of the theatre in Düsseldorf saw one of these productions and invited her to work as an assistant director at his theatre, later to proceed to her own independent work. In 1993 her production of *Romeo and Juliet* opened the theatre season of the Schauspielhaus in Düsseldorf, and since then she has directed there regularly, as well as in Hamburg and Bonn. Company work has been described as her strength: with an international group of actors from nine European countries she presented *A Midsummer Night's Dream* (1995), and plans further international collaborations. More recent productions include Ionesco's *The Chairs*, Düsseldorf, 1996, *Twelfth Night* (Hamburg, 1996), and Measure for Measure (Hamburg, 1998). From 2007/8 she will serve as artistic director of the Cologne municipal theatre. (Meyer-Dinkgräfe 2002, 25).

Chapter Sixteen

The Younger Generation: Martin Woelffer

Martin Woelffer[1], of the Berlin boulevard comedy theatres, Komödie and Theater am Kurfürstendamm, in interview with DMD, 3 April 2001.

DMD
Both your theatres do not receive any subsidies, and have to get their funds from selling seats alone?

MW
Yes, there is no subsidy, and since the Wall came down, some ten years ago, it has become much more difficult for the theatres to sustain themselves. As soon as a production is not very successful, you get into debt. That happens, not only in Berlin, but in general terms, much more frequently than in earlier times. Very successful productions are not always able to make up for that debt. An additional problem is that in the context of the theatre scene in Berlin, other theatres can pay higher salaries. My father[2] tells me that this was different in the past. Then the actors would come to us from television to be able to earn good money for a change. That's changed completely: nowadays, actors get much more for work in film and television, and also at other theatres. We can't compete with that. As a result, we will have to apply for subsidies soon, if we manage to get into the system. On the other hand, our position is that we would be perfectly happy if there weren't any subsidies at all, for anyone. We would be at an advantage then, but the current situation is one of competition where the competitors are not equal, and that's too tough in a city like Berlin. It's completely different in Hamburg, where structures are the same they were ten years ago. There it's quite possible for a theatre to sustain itself financially, through ticket sales of more than ninety percent. As far as Berlin is concerned, we have the best percentage of sold tickets across the sector. But even if you have got a very good and very popular

production, you cannot expect a full house every evening. At weekends, yes. Sometimes during the week, but only if we apply our new approaches of inviting stars of the new generation, such as Katja Riemann[3]. Some years ago it would have been unthinkable for someone like that to appear on the stage of a boulevard comedy theatre, because the theatres had the image of being too outmoded, deteriorated towards popular theatre. That's what we have been trying to develop over the last few years, new audiences.

DMD
Are you also trying to re-educate the existing audiences?

MW
Yes, we have to, but it's difficult. Slowly and gradually we are successful. You mustn't hit them over the head; they have to stay as audiences. But we are quite successful in this, I think, as the figures keep telling us.

DMD
How do you generally attract your audiences? With the plays you put on, or with stars from TV and film?

MW
Primarily still with the stars. However, we did notice that TV does not make stars. They have to be film stars. TV stars come into your living room every evening anyway, and therefore it's not so exciting to see them on stage. Stars have to be true stars. The stars of the older generation, of the 1960s and 70s were known mainly from film. Occasionally, a play is the star. That happened for us with *Comedian Harmonists*[4]. It sold out from day one, and we had 400 sold out performances. Nevertheless, the aim is to make not only star theatre, especially because it becomes more and more difficult to cast stars for all your productions, with our two theatres running shows side by side.

DMD
So the plays have to be attractive as well.

MW
Exactly. We work hard at this, to do more than conventional boulevard. For example, we try to put on Ayckbourn[5]. Always a risk, in general and here in Berlin in particular. We Germans don't have this history and this gift of being able to laugh at ourselves. And you have to have this gift to

appreciate Neil Simon[6]. I have seen a number of Ayckbourn's own productions, and I am always astonished how lightweight and funny it feels. Here, on the other hand, you often get Ayckbourn as modern-day Chekhov. You will see how we deal with it tonight[7]. Here you have two actors who take themselves very seriously. We were able to attract them to our stage only because they see the play as a serious play. I doubt whether we would have been able to contract Katja Riemann for a farce. As a result, perhaps the farcical element in Ayckbourn is neglected. And we would not have been able to contract Ms Riemann either if we had been in Cologne. It has to be Berlin, it has to be Kudamm. This is the way forward for us, to approach new kinds of stars to attract new kinds of audiences to our theatres.

DMD
What is your view of the different subgenres of boulevard comedy? Do you have preferences?

MW
Well, I grew up with boulevard comedy. As a result of issues to do with generation conflicts, I developed some dislike for the somewhat narrow-minded boulevard comedy that developed in Germany in the 1960s. It was chic, and "in" in those days, and was meant to continue into the 1970s and 1980s. Over time, and by now certainly, it has become just too repetitive, and therefore the quality goes downhill. I think it is necessary for boulevard theatre to reflect its own origins. Boulevard, large street, large city, self-reflexive, but light and entertaining. Above all: quirky. That needs to be a quality of the audiences and of the stage. This quirkiness has been lacking for many years now. During the sixties and seventies, much hinged on the sets. People saw the sets and thought: that's what we would like to live in. No chance of that today any more: we are living in a state where everyone has almost fulfilled their dreams of living. As far as actors are concerned, they play not the situation, but for the effect on the audience. The latter is nothing bad in itself if they also play the situation. That's why I appreciate that boulevard has to open up, to include musical entertainment or entertainment in the widest sense.

DMD
One problem you face may be the lack of new blood German dramatists in the genre.

MW
Yes, indeed. There must be some around, but I don't know them.

DMD
Pillau[7] and Flatow[8] are older

MW
Yes. But younger authors who write comedies that are not just very funny with every line, but where there is a hero in a precarious situation, where things remain humane, don't exist. Some people do try, we get quite a number of new scripts, but they merely copy Flatow, and it gets really petit-bourgeois, lacking genuine humour. Sometimes a really good comedy ends up on our desks, but often not from Germany.

DMD
In the UK, we have Cooney[9] and Chapman[10], technically brilliant, but

MW
Flat

DMD
Yes, lacking human warmth. All mechanical, next punch line, please. Audiences roaring with laughter and asking themselves afterwards what they have been laughing about.

MW
Ok, but in Germany we'd be happy to have someone who at least understands the mechanics.

DMD
Against that background, how do you put together your season repertoire?

MW
We do try to follow a certain system, and at the moment it seems to work quite well. In the one theatre we have the kind of comedy that our conventional audiences have enjoyed for years. And in the other theatre we have a more demanding play, Ayckbourn. But the major concern when putting together our seasons is to see who is available when. So our decisions are not always based on dramaturgical principles, because we depend too much on the stars and their availability. Who is available, when, for what play. Sometimes we find a play and think this is idea for so

and so, or someone approaches us and says I would like to play such and such with you... It always varies.

DMD

And then you have to coordinate with Hamburg and Dresden[11]?

MW

That's the aim. Dresden is different, but the exchange does work in Hamburg. They have splendid audience, they are happy about many things and are very reliable. We can confidently transfer productions that have been successful here in Berlin. Dresden is different. They have a different sense of humour, and they prefer different actors than audiences in Berlin or Hamburg. They don't know the stars from the West, so there they work with a small number of people whom nobody knows outside Dresden, and the audiences flock to the theatre to see them. So our initial plans to reduce production costs by transferring productions does not work in Dresden at all. By now they do their own season repertoire. Sometimes too independently, but by now they are quite successful. They are the second-best attended theatre in Dresden next to the Semper Opera, which is beyond competition anyway. I am a bit doubtful about the location of the Dresden Komödie, too far outside.

DMD

When you launch a production here in Berlin, do you attempt to take the entire cast to Hamburg, or only the magnets, the stars?

MW

If at all possible the entire cast. Sometimes we launch in Hamburg and transfer here.

DMD

Earlier you talked about the actors' fees. Do you pay per performance, or for weeks or months of work?

MW

Only with performance fees. Every performance is paid. We don't pay for rehearsals either.

DMD

Could you give an indication of the range of fees?

MW

I cannot mention the fees for the stars. But I could say that the budget for one performance is around 3,000 DM. That means a normal part comes to DM 300, with DM 400 or DM 500 counting as real good pay. Stars get more, based on negotiation. But we still cannot compete with stars getting DM 2,000 per performance in the Renaissancetheater or the Theater des Westens. We just cannot go higher, because all costs rise, costs for rent, for maintenance. We can only save expense when it comes to people, fees. So we have to do more, work more, we launched a touring branch of our company, most productions are sent on tour, all for the one purpose of keeping us away from going bust.

DMD

How many weeks do you schedule for rehearsals?

MW

Depending on the production, between five to seven weeks. On average six days a week. We have rehearsal rooms here on site, on large and one small.

DMD

Over the last few years, many boulevard comedy theatres in Germany were founded. Do you see this genre as a need of our times?

MW

Yes, most certainly. I think that boulevard theatre is a kind of theatre, at least in Germany, that has not been exploited fully yet. In times of increased hardship, people want more entertainment

DMD

How would you describe the hardship Germany is facing at the moment?

MW

Good question. I think you need to place the word in quotation marks. There is of course more unemployment. As far as Berlin is concerned, there has been a wave of lack of orientation since the fall of the Wall. Who am I, where do I want to go, and where does all this lead in this particular city. This kind of fear has turned into a pseudo-fear. People saying "I've got so many problems". All this despite the fact that you really cannot complain about poverty in Germany. But still people think that there are more chances now of falling into poverty. That's a kind of burden for people, some kind of pressure.

DMD
What you just said reminds me of friends I have in Germany who tell me "I've got this great job, but without exaggeration it could happen that the boss comes tomorrow and makes me redundant."

MW
Yes, there is a kind of fear, inherent, not expressed. Might actually be quite helpful to regenerate creativity. In our context of boulevard theatres, creativity went dormant, because it always worked, automatically. When I was younger, there was no doubt that every evening would be sold out. That was the state of affairs for decades. We were stunned when a performance was not sold out. And the other theatres flourished because they got subsidies.

Notes

1 and 2
The two boulevard comedy theatres in Berlin, almost adjacent to each other on Berlin's major 'boulevard', the Kurfürstendamm, are the oldest boulevard comedy theatres in Germany. The Kurfürstendamm-Theater opened in 1922 with a production of Curt Goetz's *Ingeborg*, with Goetz himself (1888-1960) and Adele Sandrock (1863-1937) in the cast. In 1924, Max Reinhardt (1873-1943) asked the architect Oskar Kaufmann (1873-1956) to build the Komödie in the mode of a castle theatre; the opening production was Goldoni's *Il servitore di due padroni* (Servant of Two Masters). In 1927, dramatist Ferdinand Bruckner took over the Kurfürstendamm-Theater, which was renamed Theater am Kurfürstendamm, followed in 1928 by Reinhardt, who asked the same architect who had built the theatre, Kaufmann, for major refurbishments. In 1932, Reinhardt withdrew from the Theater am Kurfürstendamm and for the 1932/1933 season there were altogether six artistic directors in a row. In 1933, finally, Hans Wölffer (1904-76) took over both the Komödie and the Theater am Kurfürstendamm. In 1942, under the Nazi regime, the two theatres were nationalised; they burned down in 1943 when an allied plane was shot down and crashed nearby. The Komödie reopened in 1946, the Theater am Kurfürstendamm in 1947. The Komödie was taken over by Dr Kurt Raeck (1903-1981) in 1949, where Hans Wölffer joined him in 1950. Wölffer had the theatre refurbished and redesigned and continued as sole artistic director. In 1962, he also took over the Theater am Kurfürstendamm, which had been the home of the Freie Volksbühne from 1949 to 1962. Hans Wölffer's two sons, Jürgen and Christian, trained as actors and gained experience as actors and directors at theatres across Germany. In 1965 they joined the management of the two Berlin boulevard comedy theatres, which they took over after their father's

death in 1976. Jürgen Wölffer's son Martin, who chooses to spell his name Woelffer, is the third generation of the Wölffer family involved in the artistic management of the theatres. He took over the general artistic management from his father and uncle in 2004. Both theatres have been refurbished several times since the 1960s and the Wölffers opened newly built boulevard comedy theatres in Hamburg—the Komödie Winterhuder Fährhaus (established 1988) — and Dresden, Komödie Dresden (established 1996) (http://www.theater-am-kurfuerstendamm.de/). (Meyer-Dinkgräfe 2005, 13) At the time of writing, both Wölffer theatres in Berlin are threatened by closure because the owners, a German bank, want to build a shopping arcade where the theatres now stand. They initially terminated their contract with the Wölffers as of 31 December 2006. A well supported local and national campaign led to extension of the contract until 30.6.2007

3 Katja Riemann (b. 1963), German stage and film actress

4 Gottfried Greiffenhagen and Frank Wittenbrink's revue *Veronika, der Lenz ist da* has been one of the most popular productions at boulevard comedy theatres since its premiere in 1997 in Berlin, directed by Martin Woelffer. It is a biographical play about the members of the *Comedian Harmonists*, a band of six men—five vocalists and a pianist, who rose to fame in 1928 but were forced out of existence as a result of Nazi politics by 1934. Since its phenomenal success in 1997, the actors recruited by the Berlin boulevard comedy theatres for the production of a play initially scheduled to run for the usual two to three months, have repeatedly got back together for revivals of the play, both in Berlin and on tour. They formed the *Berlin Comedian Harmonists* and have been similarly successful on a number of tours across Germany with a repertory of songs from the original Comedian Harmonists. The group's and the production's success, are due to the feelings of nostalgia they stir in the audience.(Meyer-Dinkgräfe 2005, 76)

5 Alan Ayckbourn (b. 1939), leading British writer of comedy.

6 Neil Simon (b. 1927), leading American dramatist.

7 Horst Pillau (b. 1932) is one of the leading dramatists in Germany writing in the popular theatre and boulevard comedy theatre genres.

8 Curth Flatow (b. 1920). He is the most well-known and popular representative of boulevard comedy. Flatow has to date written more than twenty plays for this genre. Since 1950 he has also been active writing for film, radio and television.

9 Ray Cooney is one of the leading writers of farce in the UK today.

10 John Chapman (b. 1927) is a leading writer of farce in the UK.

11 In 1988, the Komödie Winterhuder Fährhaus, Hamburg, and in 1996, the Komödie Dresden were founded under the Wölffer management. See interview with the Dresden artistic director, Gerd Schlesselmann, in Chapter Eighteen of this book.

Chapter Seventeen

Attention to the Local: Christa Bode

Christa Bode[1] in interview with DMD, 6 April 2003.

CB

If we go back to the planning, which we have to do two years in advance, it has to do with several factors. One the one hand we see ourselves in constructive competition with the state theatre here in Stuttgart. On the other hand Stuttgart has a very vibrant scene of off-theatre. This means that the Altes Schauspielhaus and the Komödie im Marquardt have to find their distinct profiles in this city. Because we do not work with a permanent company but as a matter of principle only with guests, with contracts for a particular production, it is of mutual interest to make these contracts as early as possible. And we have to decide our seasons in time so that other theatres here in Stuttgart don't take away from us, so to speak, especially exciting plays, new plays.

DMD

You said you work only with guests. What are your criteria of selecting these? Looking at your season brochure for the Komödie, I did not see any of the big names from television, whom you would find on the stages of the boulevard comedy theatres in Berlin or Düsseldorf, for example.

CB

That is correct. My husband said goodbye very early on to the big names and put his emphasis on company work. We do work with guests, but I like to call it a freelance permanent company. Because our guests are coming back to play here again and again. Theatre is always something local. Touring productions are beyond the local, but with a permanent building a theatre has, in principle, a local impact. Theatre achieves this local impact, at least in part, by working with actors who come back again and again. Thus, audience favourites emerge. Now what about the big names? Of course there were many more of them some 30 to 40 years ago, audiences knew the faces from the bog screen and from the important theatres, Schillertheater, or Burgtheater. Just look at *Sissi*[2], there you can see half the company of the Burgtheater. Today you would look a little surprised if a Burgtheater actor would perform boulevard. Times change. Today if you ask someone, "what's your profession" and they answer "actor", you get the additional questions "stage actor or film actor". The same with agencies. Some thirty years ago you were classified as an actor. You knew your trade, had learnt it on the stage, and had also gained experience in front of the camera. Nowadays, the young actors did not have the stage as their mother, so to speak, they came directly into soaps or film, and when the time has come to remember the theatre, then they are facing a difficult situation. Whereas those who did their apprenticeship in the theatre have it easier to shift genres.

DMD
How would you then, in this framework, describe your season repertoire? What are your criteria when putting a season together?

CB
I said earlier that theatre has got something to do with local impact, predominantly local impact, and as a result we repeatedly have a play in Swabian dialect in the Komödie's repertoire. This evening you will see an example, *Oh Sippschaft*, which is an adaptation of two comedies by Ludwig Thoma[3], *Dichterlorbeer* and *Die Kleinen Verwandten*, transported into a Swabiaxn milieu, quite well done, I hope you will enjoy it. We are looking for an adaptation of playable pieces which entertain the people, but which also come on the basis of a literary original. Some years ago, we thus had Goethe's *Mitschuldigen*, which the same author transposed into Swabian, under the title *Selber Schuld*. The main character was played by Walter Schultheiss, another actor who grew up with the theatre, and who belongs to the stars here in Swabia, and it was a very good success. But I should say clearly that if this local star had not been part of it, I don't think the Swabians would have dared come close to *Mitschuldigen* by Goethe, in the Komödie. So it is important for us to cater for the local Swabian element. But that cannot be our main aim. In addition, we are always on the lookout for new plays. Thus next season we will have another world premiere, *Eine Gute Partie* by Stefan Vögel[4], we made the contract three years ago already, it's still the world premiere, and in joint forces with Felix Bloch Erben[5] we think it's a very good play. But in comparison with

comedy theatres in Munich and Düsseldorf and Berlin, who often work
with stars, the subject matter is more critical. The plays is about an old,
gnarled man, a widower, who lives his life in his flat, almost all by
himself, and all his diversion is an old mate of his who visits him once a
week for a game of chess. The old man's son is very worried, because he
sees that his father can't cope with the household as well as the neat son
would like. In other words, the old man is a slob. So the son says: "Papa,
things can't go on like this, we have to change something here". And he
hires a housekeeper. He has chosen a very young thing and the old man
manages with ease to chase away all the young housekeepers whom his
son brings. Until Rosalinde Hundsheimer faces up to the challenge. Yes,
that's her name, and she is not that young any more either. I won't reveal
more for now. But it does take place in a slightly different kind of milieu.
It's a kind of everyday milieu, just as with Sabine Thiesler's *Lottoglück*,
also with simple people, which can bring the benefit of people recognising
themselves on stage. We want this kind of play in the Komödie im
Marquardt in Stuttgart, but just as well we want to have the "door open,
door close" farce, this year we have *Othello darf nicht Platzen*[6]. We also
put American entertainment into the next season, which dominates the
market especially as far as new plays are concerned. We always tried to
include Pillau[7], Flatow[8], Goetz[9], Thiesler[10], Kohlhase[11] and to thus cover
the German-speaking section, but there is not much by way of new plays
here.

DMD
Well, at least Flatow and Pillau are quite old now.

CB
Pillau still writes. We even had a world premiere of his a few years ago.
Pillau has acquired a firm place in our repertoire. The audiences like him
and accept him. But we also try to give the audiences some costume plays,
such as this year *Oh Sippschaft*, and next year *Fisch zu Viert*[12], to give our
audiences something for the eye, because comedies, in comparison with
other genres, are often very short-lived. That also relates to topicality.
Something that deals with a specific topic which we cannot present any
more some ten to fifteen years later. Sabine Thiesler, for example, wrote a
fine comedy at the beginning of the 1990s. The situation is this: one part
of a family, mother with daughter and son-in-law, live in West Germany,
and the other part of the family, the other son with his wife, on the other
side of the Berlin Wall. And suddenly the Wall is gone. And those from
the East say "Great, we move to the West". So they build an extension,

everything is made a bit larger, but nothing works out at all. Mother dies, they struggle about the inheritance. 40 years in the GDR have had their impact on the people and their ways of thinking. The same is true for the people in the West. And those two are now suddenly expected to happily merge. It all ends with the family building a wall in the living room they share. A funny, nice idea, but it's lost its bite in 2003. A good play, a German-speaking author, but the play does not "work" any more.

DMD
Do Ayckbourn[13] plays "work" here?

CB
We did do Ayckbourn here, yes. It was not too well attended, but at least better than when they did Ayckbourn at the state theatre. Personally I find Ayckbourn problematic for theatres that have the word "comedy" in their name. Ayckbourn has a specifically British humour, which I love very much, but it is not for everyone, we have to be clear about that. Especially since we are here in a very religious area.

DMD
When you say "not for everyone", are you referring to the audiences and / or to the also actors and directors?

CB
No, no. I am not talking about actors and directors. Those people do not only appear in comedy theatres, but also in state theatres, municipal theatres and regional theatres. It is more a case of how prepared the audience of a comedy theatre is to deal with this special kind of humour. I think that expectations are different for pure comedy theatres and for, say, state theatres.

DMD
That's interesting, because it reflects the problems other comedy theatres seem to have with Ayckbourn. Especially since Ayckbourn is highly regarded in Great Britain itself, similar to the typical farce writers such as Cooney[14] or Chapman[15]. Ayckbourn's own productions of his plays are precisely on the level of sophistication that should make them interesting to a boulevard comedy theatre here in Germany. But when I do see Ayckbourn in such theatres here, I understand their problems.

CB

Could it be related to the translation, with the language and with the temperament?

DMD

Certainly. Or do Germans interpret to much of the serious into Ayckbourn? Because that aspect is there, of course, in the English productions, but not dominant. I saw Laufenberg's[16] production of *Raucher / Nichtraucher*[17] in Berlin, with him and Katja Riemann[18] in the multiple parts of the play. In England the audiences were in tears with roaring laughter. In Berlin the occasional friendly giggle.

CB

OK, that's a phenomenon that you will also see when productions are exchanged between Munich and Cologne or Düsseldorf. Audiences will accept the same production, with the same cast, to different degrees. Probably they are more similar in Cologne and Düsseldorf. It all depends what kind of thing I do in which region. Because different mentalities don't just exist across the boundaries of nation states, such as Germany and Great Britain, but also within Germany. This leads back to what I said at the beginning: theatre is something local.

DMD

The Berlin management noticed that when they opened their "branch" in Dresden, which was planned to be, like Hamburg, a stage to take in the original Berlin productions. But they noticed, in Dresden, that the audiences did not want the stars from the former West, they just did not know them, they wanted stars they knew, from the former East. Fortunately the Wölffers[19] allowed their manager in Dresden to create his own repertoire, and now only the financial management for Dresden is done through the administration in Berlin.

CB

Fine, we could just as well say that the touring companies prove the opposite. But still, from experience, the intensity of audience response is different from region to region. In one place people will laugh at these lines, and in a different place they will laugh at different lines, or not at all. British humour has its problems in Germany. Not only in the theatre, but also in advertising. I love TV advertisements. A recent British ad shows someone driving in a Volkswagen Golf, or Polo, or something like that, and he drives full speed into a ditch. The car is completely demolished.

The driver gets out and says: "I am completely unharmed because of", whatever, air bag, and all the other things in that car. Such an ad for a car would be completely unthinkable in Germany. Inconceivable, to advertise the safety aspects of a car with such a morbid... Yes, it's a question of mentality, and people are trained to accept American mentality, through films, through soaps, the flood of *Dallas* and so on. People have become much more familiar with American ways of life than with the somewhat more elegant, polite, refined that characterises the British. That's why I emphasise, again, the local function of theatre. Including local dialect. Not exclusively, but as one element. Also because, in the context of globalisation and its mixing of languages, which have been described as growing flexibility, by using dialect we can provide roots for the people. What are people, after all, without roots? They drift somewhere, anywhere, like a flag in the wind, like a dandelion. For people, roots, identity, character, are part of life, mould and provide stability.

Notes

1 Christa Bode is the wife of Elert Bode, who was the artistic manager of the Komödie im Marquardt and the Altes Theater, Stuttgart, from 1976-2002. She served as her husband's personal assistant towards the end of his tenure at the theatre.

2 Elisabeth Eugenie Amalie von Wittelsbach (1837-1898) was Empress of Austria and Hungary. She was allegedly called Sisi (possibly misread from Lisi). Film director Ernst Marischka directed a film trilogy, *Sissi* (1955), *Sissi-Die Junge Kaiserin* (1956) and *Sissi-Schicksalsjahre einer Kaiserin* (1957) about her life. The main characters of the film were played predominantly by actors employed at the Vienna Burgtheater.

3 Ludwig Thoma (1867-1921), German writer who gained popularity through his funny and insightful descriptions of Bavarian life.

4 Stefan Vögel (b. 1969), Austrian dramatist, representing the much-needed younger generation of comedy writers.

5 Felix Bloch Erben is a leading publisher in Germany specialising in otherwise unpublished scripts of stage plays. They usually serve as authors' agents as well, distributing copies of the scripts for production to theatres and collecting royalties on the authors' behalf.

6 German title of *Lend me a Tenor*, by Ken Ludwig.

7 Horst Pillau (b. 1932) is one of the leading dramatists in Germany writing in the popular theatre and boulevard comedy theatre genres.

8 Curth Flatow (b. 1920). He is the most well-known and popular representative of boulevard comedy. Flatow has to date written more than twenty plays for this genre. Since 1950 he has also been active writing for film, radio and television.

9 Curt Goetz (1888-1960), German actor, director and dramatist, one of the wittiest writers of and actors in comedy.

10 Sabine Thiesler (b. 1957) is a German writer for stage and television.

11 Wolfgang Kohlhaase (b. 1931), German dramaturg, script writer and dramatist.

12 The title translates as *Fish for Four*, written by Wolfgang Kohlhaase and Rita Zimmer.

13 Alan Ayckbourn (b. 1939), leading British writer of comedy.

14 Ray Cooney is one of the leading writers of farce in the UK today.

15 John Chapman (b. 1927) is a leading writer of farce in the UK.

16 Eric Uwe Lauffenberg (b. 1960), German actor, director and artistic director.

17 The German title for *Intimate Exchanges*

18 Katja Rieman (b. 1963), German stage and film actress

19 The Wölffer family founded and still manage the two boulevard comedy theatres in Berlin, and founded branches in Hamburg and Dresden. See interviews with Martin Woelffer and Gerd Schlesselmann (the artistic director in Dresden, 1996-2003) in Chapters Sixteen and Eighteen).

CHAPTER EIGHTEEN

THE MANAGER:
GERD SCHLESSELMANN

Gerd Schlesselmann[1] in interview with DMD, 4 April 2001

DMD
The Komödie Dresden was founded in 1996. Is it successful?

GS
Better from year to year. But it is very difficult, because it is not easy to understand the people in Dresden and predict what they will be doing. I mean, today you can't predict any audience, and particularly so here in Dresden. There is a saying that what the people in Dresden don't know, they won't go to. And they really heed that. So working here has been a real tightrope walk. This led to this house working almost independently of Berlin, by now. Mr Wölffer's[2] original idea, that we become, like Hamburg, let me put it quite cruelly, a place where they merely shift their Berlin productions to make money, disappeared completely. He has accepted that. So in effect, in the current season, for example, there are only two productions in the repertoire that come from Berlin. No that's wrong, put like that: I should have said: two productions that were originally suggested by Berlin. They will be produced here first and will then transfer to Berlin, perhaps also to Hamburg. In the next season we will have only productions coming from here and performed here, which will not transfer. The actors are, at least as far as the main parts are concerned, really always former stars from East Germany. Because otherwise there is no point.

DMD
So you would not have any success here with typical comedy theatre stars from the West?

GS

No, zero. I just had a series of readings of literature, with Cornelia Froboess[3], who has quite a name, really, and Hoger[4] was here, and Christian Quadflieg[5], recently. In summer we will have Fischer-Dieskau[6]. The audience figures make you want to run away. These people would fill houses anywhere else, and here with Quadflieg we had 180 people sitting in a 643 seat theatre.

DMD

That's a luxury, then…

GS

Yes, only luxury. That's why I pursued my aim of opening a small stage, so that you can have such readings in a small space with some 99 seats. We are trialling that now. This evening, for example, we will have a production there with some 50 people in the audience. Not too bad for a new play which nobody here in Dresden has ever heard of.

DMD

And the standard repertoire, which is now your own. To what extent do you attempt to still imitate of copy the Berlin tendencies, such as trying to combine traditional boulevard comedy and more serious, more literary, demanding comedies?

GS

Actually, we only do more demanding comedy. We found, quite to our surprise, that pure boulevard does not work here at all, they flop.

DMD

Can you give an example?

GS

For example, Ayckbourn flopped. No need to try Ayckbourn again here. I tried Dario Fo, flopped. Neil Simon, so far, always flopped, with one exception. When we did *Sonny Boys*, we had one of Dresden's biggest stars playing one of the two lead characters. It sold out every day. But when he could not appear, due to illness, for a week, sales were near zero. People here are not open to new things. You have to somehow package it very cleverly. I have got one star here, you will see him later, Tom Pauls[7]. The play you are going to see him in, *Oscar* by Magnier, would not interest anyone on its own. But with Pauls in it, it's usually sold out. It's always like that in plays where he stars, I keep meticulous statistics. For example, we put on the *Olsenbande*. The film was a cult film here in the East, because it carried the looser-mentality of people here quite well. The film was hardly known in the West. We will have the 100th performance of this play soon, all sold out, which is quite an achievement. Every year we open the season with a play by Goetz[8], because that has been very successful. So our repertoire consists of well-known plays with well-known actors. Goetz, then *Feuerzangenbowle*[9], then *Harold and Maude*, then Joseph Kesselring's *Arsenic and Old Lace*. Many of those plays have been film classics in their own right. Our seasons are comparatively conservative. On that basis we can dare to present some classics. We did Molière's *Eingebildeten Kranken*[10]. I would also like to try a Shakespeare comedy here. There are no limits in that direction.

DMD
And the directors are local as well?

GS
Yes, more and more so. The last production that Mr Wölffer directed here, last December, was the flop of the year, and he was very shaken by that. Nobody was interested, and not such a great cast, either, it has to be said.

DMD
How did the Berlin management decide to open up this theatre here in Dresden in the first place?

GS
The city first wanted to build a cinema multiplex here, with three screens. That does not work out financially at all, in this location. At that time I was in communication with them about a big theatre for musicals. And the question arose in that context. I knew that Mr Wölffer wanted to open a theatre here in Dresden, I approached him and showed him the area, and so it developed. We rearranged the original planning, and were able to have it all built as we wanted it. This is why every seat has a small writing desk facility inbuilt. So we can use the theatre for congresses.

DMD
As an additional source for income.

GS

Correct. We have had some twenty-four civic initiation ceremonies here, as well as short congresses. With the large mall out there we have the additional advantage that we can feed many people at the same time. That reminds me to tell you: unlike the other Wölffer stages, we have our own catering, it belongs to us. They are all employed by us. I do not lease this. I found out in my previous theatre work that leaseholders are a disaster for a theatre. Because after half a year at the latest you have drifted apart. And then you are stuck with them for another four and a half years. And they do everything, only not what you would like them to do. Here, though, I can say I would like this like that, whatever.

DMD

And the audience like that as well, don't they?

GS

Yes, and the actors as well, they have their own table here, which is always reserved for them, and we cater for some special diets as well. So we have a kind of staff canteen here for them,

DMD

But a public canteen, so the food has to be better than at other staff only canteens…

GS

Yes, precisely.

DMD

How long is your rehearsal period?

GS

On average six weeks. We have a rehearsal stage here.

DMD

In the same building?

GS

Yes. Initially I didn't want one, I wanted to have a kind of attic. But Mr Wölffer prevailed. Today I am happy that he prevailed, because things developed differently: in earlier times there was no need for a rehearsal stage because all productions came from Berlin fully rehearsed. And now that we rehearse all productions here, it's of course good that we have our own rehearsal stage.

DMD
Otherwise things would have been more difficult...

GS
Yes, we would have had to rent somewhere.

DMD
Do you pay per evening, or for a month or production?

GS
For the evening, but I am having my thoughts about this, because we a moving in the direction of a core company, where people are involved in three to four productions, not necessarily in main parts, but anyway. For those it would be worth considering a monthly payment. Maybe it turns out to be cheaper, as well. But that's a thought for next year. Because audiences come to see specific actors, we of course try to attract those actors to our stage for two or three productions a year. So that audiences can say, oh, so and so is performing here again, let's go.

DMD
What is the range of fees per evening?

GS
With one exception he have a range up to DM 700. With that we are still adjusted to Berlin, which, too, is a private theatre that does not receive subsidies. We have to budget and cost out almost harder here than in Berlin. As a result, as far as our production costs are concerned, our house works the cheapest of all the Wölffer stages.

DMD
Perhaps also because many of the actors are living here...

GS
No, they don't, that's one of our main cost factors... They almost all live in Berlin. The NDR[11] moved away from here to Leipzig, there are no production sites here. If you are a freelance actor your only chance of being noticed is in Berlin. So all actors originally from Dresden move

there, because they think the market is more favourable for them there. So when we then want to employ actors, we have to get them from Berlin.

DMD
You have got some rented flats which you make available for the actors? As part of the contract, or do they…

GS
Yes, part of the contract.

DMD
And what kind of an audience do you have, age wise, and in comparison with Berlin?

GS
I would claim, and I can prove it, too, that we have the whole age range from young to old. A good average. That means there are also enough young people here. In contrast, the average of the other Wölffer stages if 45-50.

DMD
What is the relationship between subscription and open sale?

GS
That is still underdeveloped. Hardly measurable. Not even 10%. We sell most in open sale. We are very successful, thank God: by now we are the most well attended theatre in the East after Deutsches Theater, Volksbühne and BE.

DMD
That's indeed remarkable.

GS
And here in Dresden were are number one. We clearly marked out our place, through the diversity of what we offer. We offer an interesting program, also with all the special events, which attract other kinds of audiences. This news spreads among the artists. So that now I have artists calling me and asking whether they could appear on our stages with a guest contract. Alternatively, we approach people and ask them to come over and do a show. Groups such as *Badesalz*[12] or Sissi Perlinger[13]. Next year, for example, we have a three week guest performance from Berlin.

We make theatre for the people here from Dresden, while the Berlin boulevard comedy theatres make theatre for the tourists, as I see it. And those in Hamburg, again, make theatre for their city.

DMD
What do the other theatres here say to the competition which you represent for them?

GS
How should I put this... I have had a reasonable relationship with the artistic manager of the state theatre. This is also because he has to acknowledge me as artistic manager, because before I started here, I worked in state theatres myself, up to the level of artistic manager, but altogether initially they tried to avoid me. But they gave that up after some four years.

DMD
When they realised that he is here to stay...

GS
Yes, and they also noticed that while the actors with the state theatre sniffed at us, they now would love to perform here. They also always attend our performances. They would love me to offer them a part. But I have abandoned that idea, because with the state theatre I don't have a chance, logistically, except for special events. With regular productions it's a disaster. For example, I have got a production of *Sekretärinnen*[14] ongoing, our own production. We have actresses in it from three other theatres. And to find slots is proving a nightmare. In May we managed to find one slot. In the long run you just ruin a production that way.

DMD
It is interesting to observe that over the last 10 years, quite a number of boulevard comedy theatres were founded.

GS
Thinking back, in 1972 at the state theatre we did many more comedies at the state theatre. We had a different philosophy then. We were not shy, we thought we are making theatre for the audiences and for the city. In that context it was obvious that we did two to three comedies per years. Today the main problem is that the state theatres think that they have to direct all their productions one more crazy than the other. So much so that

sometimes even the plot does not get across to the audience. And they are surprised that the audiences stay away. I think that audiences, on the whole, when they go to the theatre, they want to be well entertained. If the theatre offers a good mix, I've got a chance to coax the audience, through good, entertaining pieces, to come and see the occasional experiment. Or I offer the experiment in a smaller venue. Because you just could not do some productions in the big house, because you did not get the house full. I worked in the largest theatre in Germany. In Hamburg, when I started there, we had 1,400 seats. If you get only 200, you've got a crisis. Fortunately, the interim artistic manager, Liebermann[15], managed to push, with the city administration, that they gave him a studio theatre. The new artistic manager, Stromberg[16], reduced the size of the main theatre to 960. They put some productions on to the back stage, with the audience sitting on the stage. Absurd. Instead of just spending some thought on what could entice people not to stare at the television but to go to the theatre. The state theatres can't solve this. That's why there is this vast potential for boulevard comedy theatres. In addition, state theatres always considered themselves too noble to do boulevard comedy.

DMD
When they do it, nobody laughs

GS
Nobody is interested. Because they can't do it. That's another problem here. You have to find directors who can work in this genre at all. They don't exist at the state theatres. Who should direct comedy there? At the state theatre in Hamburg, only Harry Maien[17] directed comedies. And occasionally Fassbinder[18]. That was sensational. We had that problem already then, that we did not have anyone capable of directing comedy. They would not stoop that low. Flimm was good at it, too. His productions of *Nackter Wahnsinn*[19] und *As You Like It* were gorgeous. But he has a completely different attitude. He notes that the number of people going to the theatre has gone down. And I can only say: rightfully so. Because what is happening in state theatres these days is deadly boring; each director wants to top the other with regard to novelty. So that the critics have more reason to praise them excessively. I don't make theatre for the six major critics in this country. I make theatre for hopefully a million people. That's why comedy theatres get more and more audiences. The same actor who does the special performance here tonight played in *Tod eines Handlungsreisenden*[20] at the state theatre, where he had only one third of the audience. Although he is one of the stars here in Dresden. The

audiences look very closely. That play is always sold out in the West. Here it was a flop. And it was a good production. If it had been a bad production, I'd have said, OK... But it was a good production.

DMD
Interesting. But it takes time to know your audience.

GS
Yes, that's why we lost money in our first two seasons. Because we started off with a completely wrong approach. You can correct such a mistake only at best medium term. The theatre was on the brink of Wölffer closing it down again. I then managed to convince him, in a couple of discussions, to allow me some more time with a new approach. It worked, and audience numbers rose. Now he allows me to do as I see fit, because he has realised that we have had rising numbers for the last four years. The artistic side of Dresden is all in our own hands. We do all ourselves, really, including the set. All we use from the Berlin setup is the staff bookkeeping. We have our own lady for marketing, who tries to get people into the theatre, both for the performances but also for congresses and so on. We can't afford posters across the city, but we put some into selected shops. Then we have our web presence, which keeps taking shape. We have a newsletter, which is sent to some 800 people by now. We also have a link to our website from the city website, where they get information and where they can also book tickets.

DMD
There's also a direct link from the ZDF Theaterkanal page.

GS
Yes, by now we are getting requests from others to allow them to put links to us onto their webpages. Recently a major hotel chain. No problem. A local newspaper did the same.

DMD
Talking about newspapers, what's your relationship with the local press, and the regional and national newspapers?

GS
The nationals do not take any notice of productions in comedy theatres

DMD
Except perhaps Berlin

GS
Yes, Berlin, but there also only if they do a world premiere

DMD
Or for Katja Riemann[21], a film star

GS
We don't even write to them any more, to invite them, there's no point. That can be quite depressing. To mobilise just the press in Dresden to attend a performance is enough work. And the reasons you hear, they give you, why someone cannot make it after all…

DMD
Those that do come, are they at least competent, independent of whether the reviews are good or bad?

GS
No, not even that. There are two or three who can write competently, but sometimes it's outrageous.

DMD
Do the editors send their major critics, or some part-time people?

GS
In most cases it's the major critics, the newspapers are too small to diversify. But in Hamburg, for example, there are some critics who attend only productions in the state theatre, and some who specialise in private theatres. That's why the reviews there are so different. The critics who go to private theatres write always in a more well-meaning manner. Nothing like that here. You can't take any of them seriously. From regional newspapers I know that they sometimes read the plays in advance, then they can integrate some knowledge about the play into their reviews. In Hamburg there are even reports about forthcoming productions. But here you have to make every effort, even for people like Quadflieg or Fischer-Dieskau.

DMD

But the audiences do not know that. How do they react to the opinion of the reviews?

GS

They don't. I want to be very clear about this: as long as I have been working in the theatre, I found that the reviews are completely irrelevant to how well the theatre is attended. If a production is really good, and the audiences like it as well, then word of mouth propaganda sets in. A good review can support that kind of propaganda, it gets known faster, more people come to see it. But if the production is liked by the audience and gets bad reviews, the reviews can be as bad as they like, people will flock to see it. In that respect critics are redundant.

DMD

In contrast to their power on Broadway...

GS

Yes, I know that as well from personal experience, a critic can close a musical. I worked for Stella[22] in earlier times. I built up Stella in Hamburg, with Mr Kurz[23]; Mr Kurz made a trip to New York. Their critics mauled the show and it closed after six days. I had warned him against going to New York. But he didn't listen and wasted 8.5 million dollars. But there a critic can end a show. Here in Germany nobody can do that. Here only the lack of an audience can end a show. You can get wonderful reviews, for example for our *Sekretärinnen*. But despite such great reviews, the response is too weak. But I do believe in that show, because it's really good. And I also believe the longer we keep it in our repertoire, the better the response will become. That's why I have planned it over the entire next season.

DMD

Do you use good reviews in your publicity?

GS

Yes, every now and then. In Hamburg we had Zadek's[24] production of *Othello*. It was trashed by the local critics, not the national ones. But the local reviews really could not have been worse. But the audience liked that production so much, it was always sold out. Simply because it had become more of a scandalous production. In the opening night the audience was really fighting, I never experienced anything like it. And after four hours of performance things really only got started. The opening night started at 10 pm, and at 2 pm the then artistic manager, Ivan Nagel[25], had a discussion with the audience from the stage for another half-hour. We organised a discussion three weeks later, and it was more than sold out. The people in Hamburg are known as party-goers and soon after the opening night you could not be seen at any party without having seen this production. Then came the summer break and after that the show was dead. It was not longer the subject of conversation at parties. We played for houses that were only two thirds full. It's the same thing here. Word by mouth propaganda counts, nothing else. Tom Pauls in *Charlies Tante*[26], we will revive it next season, we have had seventy performances. Had bad reviews.

Notes

1 The founding artistic manager of the Komödie Dresden was Gerd Schlesselmann, in office from 1996 to 2003. He worked there under the overall management of the Wölffer family in Berlin. He was born in 1942 in Hamburg; from 1972 to 1979 he was artistic manager (*Künstlerischer Betriebsdirektor*) at the Deutsches Schauspielhaus in Hamburg under artistic director Ivan Nagel and in the same position for the 1979/80 season at the Schauspielhaus Bochum with artistic director Claus Peymann. From 1980 to 1985 he served as deputy artistic director at the Deutsches Schauspielhaus in Hamburg; in that city he also developed the alternative arts venue Kulturfabrik Kampnagel. During those years he started his collaboration with Peter Brook, whose German tour of *The Man Who* he organised in 1993. From 1985 to 89 he managed the Stella Musicaltheater, which brought *Cats* to the Operettenhaus in Hamburg, *Starlight Express* to Bochum and *Phantom of the Opera* to Hamburg. From 1989 to 1991 Schlesselmann returned to the Deutsches Schauspielhaus in Hamburg as artistic leader under the artistic director Michael Bogdanov and took on the role of interim artistic director for a time. Before joining the Komödie Dresden, he served as artistic director of the Hamburger Kammerspiele for a season (Schlesselmann, 2001).
2 The Wölffer family founded and still manage the two boulevard comedy theatres in Berlin, and founded branches in Hamburg and Dresden. See the interview with Martin Woelffer in Chapter Sixteen.
3 Cornelia Froboes (b. 1943). As a child and teenager, Froboes was popular as a singer and actor in light entertainment films. She took private acting lessons in Berlin and gave her professional debut in 1963. After seasons in Braunschweig and freelance work in Berlin, Hamburg and München, she joined the Münchner Kammerspiele in 1972. Her voice, gestures and facial expression make her one of the most intensive actors of her generation, whose many roles show preference for broken, seeking and doubting women: Sonja in Chekhov's *Uncle Vanya*, Recha in Lessing's *Nathan der Weise* (*Nathan the Sage*), the title roles in Lessing's *Minna von Barnhelm* (directed by Dieter Dorn) and Wedekind's *Lulu*, Ellida Wangel in

Ibsen's *The Lady from the Sea*, Cäcilie in Goethe's *Stella*, Viola in *Twelfth Night*, and Xenia in Edward Bond's *Summer* (directed by Luc Bondy); she has worked extensively with Dieter Dorn and Thomas Langhoff. (Meyer-Dinkgräfe 2002, 92-3)

4 Hannelore Hoger (b. 1941) trained with Eduard Marcks at the Staatliche Hochschule für Musik und Darstellende Kunst in Hamburg. In 1961 she joined the company of Kurt Hübner in Ulm, where she first met Peter Zadek. She later followed him to Bremen, Stuttgart, Bochum and Hamburg, Since 1986 she has worked freelance as an actor and director. She excels in giving convincing and life-like portrayals of strong-willed, self-confident and independent women. Major parts include Anna in *Richard III* (1968), the Fool in *King Lear* (1974), the title role in Achternbusch's *Susn* (1980), Irina in Chekhov's *The Seagull* (1984), Irma in Genet's *The Balcony* (1989), and, more recently, Turrini's *Alpenglühen* (*Glowing Alps*, Berlin, 1993). (Meyer-Dinkgräfe 2002, 125-6)

5 Christian Quadflieg (b. 1945) is the son of the great German actor Will Quadflieg (1914-2003) and a renowned actor and director for the stage and screen in his own right.

6 Dietrich Fischer-Dieskau (b. 1925) was one of the leading baritone opera and Lieder singers of his time.

7 Tom Pauls (b. 1959) is an actor and cabaret artist. He trained at the Theaterhochschule Leipzig (1979-83) and worked with company of the state theatre in Dresden until 1990. Since then he has been freelance.

8 Curt Goetz (1888-1960), German actor, director and dramatist, one of the wittiest writers of and actors in comedy.

9 The English title of this film and the play is *Burnt Punch*.

10 *Le Malade Imaginaire / The Hypochondriac*

11 *NDR* stands for Norddeutscher Rundfunk, one of the public broadcasting corporations in Germany

12 *Badesalz* is the name of a comedy duo, Henrik Nachtsheim and Gerd Knebel, founded in the early 1980s.

13 Sissi Perlinger (b. 1963) is a German actress and entertainer.

14 Frank Wittenbrink wrote the musical *Sekretärinnen / Secretaries* in 2000.

15 Rolf Liebermann (1910-1999) was a Swiss composer and artistic manager of the opera houses in Hamburg (1959-1973 and 1985-88), and Paris (1973-1980).

16 Tom Stromberg (b.1960), studied German and Theatre Studies at the University of Cologne. Stages in his career in the theatre are his first post as dramaturg in Darmstadt, 1984-86, the same post, and later artistic directorships in Frankfurt (Theater am Turn) and Hamburg (Deutsches Schauspielhaus, 2000-2005).

17 Harry Maien was a German actor, stage director and dubbing director.

18 Rainer Werner Fassbinder (1945-1982), actor and film director, was one of the most influential representatives of New German Cinema.

19 *Noises Off* by Michael Frayn (b. 1933)

20 *Death of a Salesman* by Arthur Miller (1915-2005)

21 Katja Riemann (b. 1963), German stage and film actress

22 *Stella* is the name of a company that produces musicals world-wide, often in purpose-built venues.

23 Friedrich Kurz, German producer, launched the trend of purpose-built venues for large scale musicals. He was the founder of Stella, see above.

24 Peter Zadek (b. 1926). His family emigrated to Britain in 1933, where he trained at the Old Vic School in London with Tyrone Guthrie. At the Old Vic he directed a double bill of Wilde's *Salome* and Eliot's *Sweeney Agonistes*. In the 1950s he worked for the BBC and throughout Britain, culminating in a major success with Genet's *The Balcony* (1957) at the Arts Theatre Club in London. In 1958 he returned to Germany, carrying with him his love for Shakespeare, his love for boulevard, and his preference for topical provocation. In 1960 he joined Kurt Hübner in Ulm, and stayed with him in Bremen (1962-7). He was artistic director in Bochum (1972-7), later in Hamburg (Deutsches Schauspielhaus, 1985-9) and Berliner Ensemble (1993-6), where he frequently worked with Ulrich Wildgruber, Rosl Zech, Eva Mattes, and Ilse Ritter. In the 60s and 70s, many of his productions caused scandals. However, by now his interpretations Shakespeare are regarded as seminal for the reception of the classics on the German stage. There may be much shocking chaos, but there are also quiet, unpretentious productions which show Zadek as a master of psychological characterisation. (Meyer-Dinkgräfe 2002, 338)

25 Ivan Nagel (b. 1931). Born in Budapest, he studied in Zurich und Frankfurt am Main (with Theodor W. Adorno), worked as a theatre critic and dramaturg in Munich, and led the Deutsche Schauspielhaus in Hamburg (1972-79), founded the festival *Theater der Welt*, led the theatre in Stuttgart, and has been professor of aesthetics and performing arts in Berlin since 1988

26 *Charley's Aunt*, by Brandon Thomas (1850-1914)

CHAPTER NINETEEN

THE DRAMATURG:
FRANK BISCHOFF

Frank Bischoff Dramaturg at the *Komödie Kassel*, in interview with DMD, 28 October, 2003.

DMD

The *Komödie Kassel* was founded some 50 years ago. That's quite an achievement. Has it been at this venue for all those years?

FB

No, as far as I know the theatre's history, Kassel once had a drama school, and at some point some of those who had not found employment on graduating, got together and dedicated themselves to comedy. At first they performed in a restaurant or pub, then they had a small public venue, then a container, and in 1965 they moved in here. It's a relatively small venue, with only 145 seats. Initially the Komödie had a permanent company of twelve actors; that's no longer the case. We mainly work with guest artists, apart from two permanent members. Initially they did not do only comedy here, for a long time they tried to present classics, and it seems to have worked for a while. But when the Wall came down, some funding for the regions close to the Wall was dropped, and the *Komödie* lost its share of that funding.

DMD
But you still get some subsidy?

FB
We get a little bit, yes. From the federal state of Hessen we receive some €250,000. In comparison, the state theatre in Kassel gets €25 Million from the state and the city. Thus we clearly have to finance many of our costs from ticket sales. We also do touring across the region.

DMD
How many people are there in your administration?

FB
The director of administration, who also designs and builds the sets and takes the production photos. We have an artistic director, who directs most productions. An administrator for all aspects of finance, and myself as dramaturg. I am also dealing with publicity and marketing, and I also direct.

DMD
Sounds like the absolute minimum.

FB
Yes, and we have a lady for the box office, a lady for cleaning, a technician to help with get-in and get-out, and to service lighting and sound. We have productions with an average of five performers, it's a big production when we get up to eight.

DMD
Do you work with evening fees or monthly contracts?

FB
Neither: we do production contracts, from first day of rehearsals to the final performance, also including holidays pro rata. We also pay into the pension fund for stage staff. We think this is better than not paying for rehearsals and then to add a small fee for each performance and do all this on a freelance basis.

DMD
Looking at the season repertoire, there are not many German authors.

FB
In this season we are doing a world premiere of Pierre Franckh[1]. He is an actor as well and this is his first play. A simple story, lives all from the situations, man and woman can't find each other, and finally get together after overcoming many obstacles.

DMD
Does it resemble any other plays in the genre you know

FB

Not really, although of course ultimately the structures are very similar. In many cases there are love situations, there are many writers, painters, actors as characters, sometimes doctors, and most of these plays take place in the living room. All geared for entertainment. These plays are not meant to provide a critique of society. Sauvil's *La Surprise* (*The Surprise, Die Überraschung*) is an exception in that context. The situation is not one of love, but the play deals with the differences of rich and poor, how to make a fortune by cheating. I was happy to see this play in our season. We are planning to do another play by Sauvil[2] next season, about politicians. Sauvil is hardly known in Germany, he has written some four or five plays. The first was *Soleil pour Deux* (*Sun for Two, Sonne für Zwei*). Our artistic director, Roland Heitz[3], did the first German production of that some time ago, elsewhere.

DMD

Do you have plans to take up plays by Stefan Vögel[4]?

FB

No. It's not that easy. The *Komödie* here has assumptions about its audience, and I don't know whether those assumptions are correct. The audiences are assumed to be quite old, and there is a lack of younger audiences. We are trying to get new audiences by putting on a revue of the 1970s, *Hossa*, full of songs from the 1970s, and it worked quite well. But to keep this new audience is more difficult. We will give them a new play by Sabine Thiesler[5], *Lottoglück* (*Winning the Lottery*).

DMD

Do you have Flatow[6], or Gunter Beth[7] or Folker Bohnet[8] in your repertoire?

FB

We had Flatow's *Rock und Bluse* (*Skirt and Blouse*) some years ago, and it came across quite well. And we had a play by Beth, and one by Frank Pincus[9], and Pillau[10], we are doing one of his plays next season as well. We also did Ayckbourn[11], one of his plays was the first production Mr Heitz directed here. People keep saying that Ayckbourn is too intellectual. It should be done at municipal theatres and not at a comedy theatre

DMD

Do you have a subscription system?

FB

We have a opening night subscription, which is quite small, but nobody developed a genuine subscription system. There are some organisations to which you pay a little bit and they get you tickets. Then the city of Kassel supports theatre evenings for senior citizens. But we have to be careful not to be placed in that corner, that as a boulevard comedy theatre we do only light entertainment for senior citizens. For that reason I also worked hard to get some youth theatre going.

DMD

What is the theatre's relationship to the media, the newspapers?

FB

My personal relationship is very good. The state theatre with opera, ballet, orchestra concerts, theatre, is always in the limelight. We have an opening night every five to six weeks, which makes it difficult to maintain interest. When we do get reviews, the plot summaries clearly dominate, not so much on the achievements of the actors.

DMD

How would you describe any differences of doing a comedy at a municipal or state theatre, and at a comedy theatre?

FB

In my opinion, there is no difference. It is theatre, and a comedy needs very precise work. They are all about situations on the stage, characters on the stage, you tell a story, and that's the same for a classic and for a comedy. The wit of comedy comes from the intruder, open door, close door, the development of misunderstandings. You don't have to do that in an exaggerated way.

DMD

The casts do not have stars to attract audiences, am I right?

FB

Yes, we emphasise the achievement of the company;

DMD

How long is the rehearsal period?

FB
On average five weeks,. Sometimes six. We rehearse in the mornings on the set of the performances we have in the evenings. Only during the last week of rehearsals before the opening night do the actors get the production set and the costumes, light, sound etc., so we have a few days without evening performances before a new show opens.

Notes

1 Pierre Franckh, German actor, who shot to fame when he appeared in an episode of a weekly crime programme *Der Komissar*, aged 16. He now also directs, produces film and writes.

2 Pierre Sauvil was born in Paris and studied philosophy, before beginning to write for radio, television and the theatre. His *Soleil pour deux* plays on the generation gap, with the exchanges between established doctor and bachelor Dr. Bertholin and young, independent, eccentric Josiane Desrumeaux. She jumps into Dr. Bertholin's house through the window, claiming to be an ex-patient whom he diagnosed wrongly and says that she has come to blackmail him into giving her room and board for an indefinite time. Later she reveals herself to be his daughter. In Sauvil's *La Surprise* it is extravagant and extraordinary student Virginie Dumesnil who brings new life into the run-down marriage of Catherine and Philippe Chabrier. (Meyer-Dinkgräfe 2005, 55)

3 Roland Heitz took over the artistic management of Komödie Kassel in 2001, which had been founded in 1950. His most immediate predecessors were Horst Lateika, in office from 1987 to 2000 and Gerhard Fehn, who served for only the 2000/2001 season. Heitz trained at the Hochschule für Kunst und Theater in Saarbrücken (1976-79) and worked as an actor in Regensburg, Krefeld / Mönchengladbach, Hannover, Zurich and Hamburg. In Hamburg he added directing to his credits. At the beginning of the 1990s Heitz was artistic leader and manager at the Altonaer Theater in Hamburg. From 1995 - 98 he was deputy artistic manager at the Stadttheater Herford. In addition, he directed freelance in Münster, Bremen, Detmold, Erfurt, Wien, at the dome festival in Gandersheim and at the Torturmtheater Sommerhausen, which is led by Veit Relin (http://www.komoediekassel.de/intro.html). Heitz's term of office ended with the 2004/5 season. (Meyer-Dinkgräfe 2005, 24-25)

4 Stefan Vögel (b. 1969), Austrian dramatist, representing the much-needed younger generation of comedy writers.

5 Sabine Thiesler (b. 1957) is a German writer for stage and television.

6 Curth Flatow (b. 1920). He is the most well-known and popular representative of boulevard comedy. Flatow has to date written more than twenty plays for this genre. Since 1950 he has also been active writing for film, radio and television.

7 Gunter Beth (b. 1945), German theatre actor, director and dramatist, working predominantly in the boulevard comedy genre.

8 Folker Bohnet (b. 1937), German theatre actor, director and dramatist, working predominantly in the boulevard comedy genre.

9 Frank Pinkus (b.1958), German dramatist.

10 Horst Pillau (b. 1932) is one of the leading dramatists in Germany writing in the popular theatre and boulevard comedy theatre genres.

11 Alan Ayckbourn (b. 1939), leading British writer of comedy.

PART III:

ACADEMIA, THEORY AND PRACTICE

Chapter Twenty

Academic, Playwright, Actor and Director: David Ian Rabey

David Ian Rabey[1] (DIR) in interview with DMD, August/September 2006

DMD
You are both an academic and a theatre artist. How did those two sides of your work develop in relation to each other?

DIR
When I began my studies, initially as a BA student of English at Birmingham University, I started writing short stories, initially in response to a first year class exercise in Close Reading and Composition. With the enthusiastic encouragement of my seminar leader, K. M. Green, I persisted in writing, and followed fiction writing courses at the Arvon Foundation's Lumb Bank centre, where my tutors included Angela Carter, and at the University of California, Berkeley (as part of my second MA), where my tutors included Leonard Michaels. I published nothing, but enjoyed writing, and was working gradually towards amassing a collection of stories. Two years into my appointment as a Lecturer in Drama at the University of Wales, Aberystwyth, my department's course in Creative Writing for the Stage lacked a leader and was considered for closure, but I offered to take it over and keep it running. I had encountered various forms of tutorship of creative writing, and thought it wouldn't be impossible to apply at least some propositions and exercises to stage writing. Of course, I soon began to work out some of the important differences, challenges and pleasures of writing for stage performance, and eventually began writing a script for myself, building up from some of the speech-writing exercises which I set my students. I should also add that I had been a keen performer and director with Stourbridge Youth Theatre since my mid-teens, and thereafter at university. But in my late teens and

early twenties I didn't write anything more substantial for the stage than some student review sketches and a brief comic play (called *All's Lost in a Winter's Nightmare*, a Christmas pantomime for my fellow Shakespeare Institute MA students) which I also directed.

DMD

How would you describe the kind of dramatists and topics of drama and the related modes of theatre you favour, in relation to the books you have written and are writing, in relation to the kinds of departmental and *Lurking Truth* productions you choose to direct, and in relation to the plays you write?

DIR

I prefer speculative drama, and indeed fiction, which identifies, anatomises and challenges political pressures in profoundly imaginative terms. I think the speculative in literature, performance and other art forms represents the most distinctive development of the twentieth century. Of course there are important examples of this in earlier ages by important writers such as Shakespeare, Milton and Swift. But I think there is an important further flowering of this impulse, influenced by Surrealism. This is perhaps most innovatively manifested in drama and theatre by the work of Beckett (and in fiction by other writers I discovered whilst a university student, Joyce and Burroughs). Mimetic social realism, which deals in the observation of literal surfaces, is, for me, insufficiently theatrically incisive and compelling to engage with this task. Social realism can work well in television drama and journalism, but I believe theatre is an insistently physically and linguistically poetic medium, which can deal in vision as well as observation. So I favour drama which works in terms of what Brendan Kennelly[2] terms nightenglish which reaches beyond reason in its surprising and speculative interrogative presences, rather than the dayenglish of rational communication and explanation which is usually predicated on some utilitarian terms, beyond those of the theatre itself. I applaud Artaud's impulses, which of course have the most deeply, anarchically political consequences when you try to realise them even partly. David Rudkin[3] has rightly observed that the work I write and direct addresses and animates what lies underneath the historical tapestry, that which has been, and/or is, purposefully excluded from the official (that is, political) terms of definition.

Two nights ago my friend the writer David Thorpe[4] was proposing to me (in some words which he has since put on his website) that the philosophy and visual tradition of Surrealism and Dadaism represented the only sane responses for witnesses of the tragic chasm that exists as a tectonic rift between the parallel paths during the last hundred years of the scientific and technological developments on the one hand and human political misgovernment on the other. He was pointing out that whereas mainstream literature, particularly in Britain, tends to concentrate on pitiful single dramas of isolated alienated individuals, there is a less "respectable" and widely respected tradition of work – expressionism, fantasy, science fiction, the best comics and graphic novels – which reflects at least some aspects of the surreal and employs the imagination to objectivise aspects of our present condition which we may find too painful or difficult to explore deeply in other, more so-called "realistic" terms. I think one of the most distinguishing features of art is its ability to dissolve conventional polarities on the one hand, and explode conventional associations on the other, and this is manifested in the surreal, the metaphorical, the poetic and the theatrical. And I frequently want my plays and productions to have the visual anti-naturalistic haunting starkness of the work of the most surrealist comic and graphic novel illustrators such as Steve Ditko[5] and Dave McKean[6].

DMD
My response to the work you write and the work you direct is that I would describe it as "dark", even if it takes the form of (in your writing), or deals with (in your directing) comedy. Would you like to comment on this response / description / impression?

DIR
This may well be true. It may be linked to my sense of what constitutes imaginative responsibility in initiating and formalizing speculations and confronting possible human consequences. I am drawn to dystopian rather than utopian fantasy, and to Juvenalian (rather than Horatian) satiric impulses of confrontation which are likely to leave their audience in a state of questioning and unease, rather than permit a more conventional resolution or ease. I am certainly not averse to comedy and wit in the theatre, or indeed any other art form, but I find some forms of comedy and wit more interesting than others. I would say here that wit is here a perception of connections between otherwise disparate elements, and differences between ideas, characters and situations which are more conventionally associated. However I dislike the sort of ironic comedy which cultivates in the audience a flattered superiority, say in a condescending relation to the social mores and presumptions of an earlier historical period; I think it is inevitable, fortunate and, indeed, comic how

the passage of time demonstrates the limitations of the strictures of human awareness in any specific age, but I would proceed from the different vantage point, and take courage from the conviction, that our own age will be exposed as similarly misleaded and misleading in its social and cultural presumptions of "enlightenment" and "progress". David Thorpe was also telling me that a central principle of Dadaism is that rejection and gallows humour are legitimate responses to the absurd atrocities generated by the so-called developed world's way of life. My favourite comic dramatist is the recently deceased Peter Barnes[7], whose work masterfully demonstrates how to juxtapose incongruities to electric, surprising effects. I like Barker's[8] ideal (expressed in the performance poem *Don't Exaggerate*) of the audible laugh in the theatre which expresses individual surprise and disbelief, not a unison of superiority: not the 'gesture of solidarity' or 'gurgle of vanity', but 'the irresistible collapse of words / Before the spectacle of unbidden truth'. This can occur in good productions of work by Barnes, Barker, Beckett, Charles Wood, Shakespeare – including *Titus Andronicus* – and I would hope in moments in productions of my own theatre writing too. I'm not sure how 'dark' this is; I think it is a mark of vitality, albeit sometimes a paradoxical and courageous vitality, which may be one of the most important distinguishing qualities of comedy, art and theatre.

DMD

At the current state of your career, how would you describe the relationship between theory and practice? Is one of them dominant? How do they influence each other in your playwri(gh)ting, directing and acting, and in your academic writing?

DIR

The demands of what might, appropriately in this context, be termed my "day job" inevitably tend to take precedence: the busyness of exposition and explanation in teaching students, the placating of bureaucratic demands which are, once more, predicated on utilitarian terms of standardising definition and justification rather than educational terms of encouraging questions, all I suppose in the service of the (sometimes heartwarmingly) ludicrous attempt to make a living and raise a family. But then there is the nightwork, in individual imaginings or interpersonal encounters and rehearsal, which yields its own promptings, and becomes resentful if denied for too long. Theory and practice are different wings of my thinking and activity, which fortunately – and properly – have mutually informative contact points.

    Let me approach this from another direction. I would say that the most
direct and profound influence on my imagining and work is the
complexities of music. In rehearsal, I will use music to assist performers in
accessing emotion, and in discovering surprising rhythms. I am also, as a
director, usually trying to identify and fine-tune the music of a play, and I
think it's useful to think of plays, productions and performances in
musical terms, such as variations, reprises and deviations. My sense of
music here is not just to do with hearing the spoken language, but how this
is counterpointed with the rhythms of physicality, and sound and lighting.
My admiration for the work of certain dramatists (and directors) is not
only for the ideas and feelings they raise, but for the complex musicality
of their work. Anne Bogart rightly says the theatre practitioner is an
architect of space and time. And I will often prepare myself for writing by
playing selected music to establish or recall a mood. Occasionally this is
rock music, but contemporary original jazz composition is particularly and
increasingly influential on me. The most direct examples of this can be
seen in my collaborative work with Paula Gardiner.
    Paula is a jazz composer, for her own band and for theatre companies,
and Head of Jazz Studies at the Royal Welsh College of Music and
Drama. I had admired her work as performer and composer for some time
and commissioned her to write for my first play, *The Back of Beyond*,
staged in 1996. For that, Paula wrote and recorded a number of themes
with evocative but non-specific titles; I actually used these (as scene links
and underscorings) at points different from those for which they had been
originally conceived by Paula, but she found their relocations surprisingly
effective. My second written play, *The Battle of the Crows* (written 1996,
staged 1998), actually took its starting point of mood, and also its title,
from one of Paula's compositions, with her permission, and additional
recordings. My third piece of writing for the stage, *Bite or Suck* (written
and staged 1997), was different in that I didn't see images, I heard two
voices, and had no detailed sense of the accompanying physical
choreography. I also wanted, just for once, to explore the experience of
performing in my own writing, and so engaged Andy Cornforth[9] to direct
the play. My stage adaptation of J. G. Ballard's *Crash* featured an original
musical score composed and recorded by Eric Schneider, posted to me in
instalments which accompanied and informed my own writing. Then came
the double bill of one-person plays, *Lovefuries*. The first of these, *The
Contracting Sea*, was written specifically for the Irish performer
Antoinette Walsh[11]. I conversed with Antoinette about emotions she might
wish to address, and evocative presences and landscapes. I subsequently
awoke with the title and the sound of her voice pitched against Paula

Gardiner's double bass in a pas de deux, with the bass representing the depths of the sea. The rest of the text followed subsequently, also emerging mysteriously from dreaming and half-waking states, the last half in a torrent of sudden almost automatic writing at 6am one Sunday morning. Most of the accompanying physical choreography was discovered and developed in rehearsal. The accompanying piece, *The Hanging Judge*, was intended for a Welsh male performer, and emerged from a nightmare, in which a figure circled and chanted doggerel at a central hanging effigy in a black mass of voodoo exorcism. This time I had some ideas of movement and predominantly of rhythm (associated with the energy of doggerel), but the details of the choreography were again developed in and over three rehearsal periods for different performances, firstly with Gareth Potter[12], and secondly and thirdly with Roger Owen[13].

I would say that the ambition and musicality of my plays have been identifiably encouraged by those of Shakespeare, Howard Barker, David Rudkin, Peter Barnes, John Arden and Caryl Churchill. The more open forms of the texts of *Lovefuries* and *Crash* were also licensed by Martin Crimp's *Attempts on her Life* and Sarah Kane's *Crave* and *4:48 Psychosis*, though *Bite or Suck* was an example of the open form that predated my encounters with these plays; and I think aspects of Kane's visceral self-searching informed *Lovefuries* more deeply, particularly *Judge*. Part of the challenge of composition for me has also been to do with finding and exploring different forms: *The Back of Beyond* and *The Battle of the Crows* involving around a dozen performers each, *Bite or Suck* is a two-hander, *Crash* for an unspecified collective, *Sea a pas de deux* for performer and musician, *Judge* a (ventriloquistic, schizophrenic) solo performance.

Notes

1 David Ian Rabey (b. 1958). Formerly lecturer in English & Drama, Trinity College, Dublin. Educated at Universities of Birmingham and California, Berkeley. Artistic Director of Lurking Truth Theatre Company/Cwmni Gwir Sy'n Llechu, for whom he has written the plays *The Back of Beyond* (1996), *The Battle of the Crows* (1996) – published by Intellect Press as *The Wye Plays* (2004) - *Bite or Suck* (1997) and *Lovefuries* (*The Contracting Sea* and *The Hanging Judge*) (2004). Performance work includes title role in Barker's *Uncle Vanya* at Theatr Clwyd and Theatr y Castell, Aberystwyth; and Isonzo in Barker's production of *The Twelfth Battle of Isonzo*, in Dublin (2001), and on tour in Ireland and Wales (2002). Departmental directing work includes *The Sons of Light, The Europeans, Titus Andronicus, Coriolanus, Heartbreak House, Dreaming, Saint's Day Ursula:*

Fear of the Estuary, *The Master and Margarita* and *Gertrude—The Cry*. External directing includes work in Aberystwyth, Cardiff, Swansea and Dublin: *That Slidey Dark* by Nigel Wells (1994), *The Back of Beyond* (1996), *The Battle of the Crows* (1998), an exploratory theatricalisation of J. G. Ballard's novel *Crash* (2001) and *Lovefuries* (2004). He is an Associate of Howard Barker's theatre company, The Wrestling School, and is currently preparing a second expository study of Barker's theatre work, as well as writing on the plays of Ed Thomas, and trying to write some more of his own.

http://www.aber.ac.uk/tfts/staff/profiles/ddr.html

2 Brendan Kennelly (b. 1936) is a poet and Professor of Modern Literature at Trinity College Dublin.

3 James *David* Rudkin (b. 1936) is a dramatist. Royal Shakespeare Company staged his first play *Afore Night Come* in 1962, as part of an 'experimental season'. Without violating its social realist form, the play suggests destructive and creative cosmologies and rites lurking beneath the superficial civilisation of the English Black Country. *Cries from Casement as his Bones are Brought to Dublin* (1971), broadcast by BBC radio and staged by the RSC, develops a dramatic grappling with Anglo-Irish relations and sexual identity (Rudkin is himself half Irish), pursued in more microscopic form in *Ashes* (1973). His major plays, *The Sons of Light* (1975), *The Triumph of Death* (1981) and *The Saxon Shore* (1986), are troubling, complexly romantic, mythic explorations of identity in social crisis, with characteristic reference to imperialism, religion, the animal savagery of instinct, and the darkest recesses of sexuality. The experiences of his Promethean protagonists testify to Rudkin's sense that hope lies in the imaginative abilities of each individual to recreate myth in their own individual terms. Whilst he has maintained a consistent level of activity with radio drama and television and cinema screenplays, including work as translator and adaptor, a reappraisal of his continuingly daring original work for the stage is overdue. (Meyer-Dinkgräfe 2002, 261)

4 David Thorpe is a novelist (*Hybrids*, 2007) and environmental journalist. He is also a designer and runs his own company, Cyberium. In his 'spare' time he writes songs, music and makes pictures. See http://www.blogger.com/profile/10930421

5 Steve Ditko (b.1927) is an American comic book artist and writer. He is the co-creator of the Spiderman character.

6 Dave McKean (b. 1963) is a British illustrator, photographer and comic book artist.

7 Peter Barnes (1931-2004), was a British dramatist

8 Howard Barker (b. 1946) History (which Barker read at the University of Sussex in Brighton), not for its own sake but used as a metaphor, dominates his dramatic output, such as *Love of a Good Man* (1978) set during the First World War, or *The Europeans*, set in the aftermath of the liberation of Vienna from Islamic forces, written in 1984 and first performed in 1993. In *Uncle Vanya* (1995), Barker offers a new version of Chekhov's famous original, emphasising the individual's freedom of choice. Barker plays never fail to be complex and provocative. Many are written in a densely poetic style, often focusing on the transforming character of desire, and the exploration of acts conventionally perceived as cruel, but considered in a

morally re-evaluative context of the catastrophic will to new identity. (Meyer-Dinkgräfe 2002, 21)

9 Andy Cornforth was an undergraduate student at the University of Wales Aberystwyth and proceeded to do a Ph.D. under David Ian Rabey's supervision.

10 Eric Schneider (b. 1961) attended the University of Wales, Aberystwyth and the Whitechapel Academy of Dramatic Arts. He collaborated as an actor, co-director and actor's trainer with tag poetry's production of Movements of the Mouth, double-billing Ernst Jandl's *Die Humanisten* (*The Humanists*) and *Aus der Fremde* (*From the Distance*, 1991, The Octagon, London, directed by Thomas Gruber). The same year he played Starhemberg in the world premiere of Howard Barker's *The Europeans* (Theatr Y Castell, Aberystwyth, directed by John O'Brien and David Ian Rabey). He has translated into Luxembourgeois and directed two of Barker's plays: *The Castle* (1990, Sprangfal Theater Co., Escher Schluechthaus arts centre) and *The Europeans* (1995, Théâtre d'Esch, commissioned by the theatre and Luxembourg European Cultural City). He is a founder member of the Lurking Truth and played in the world premiere of David Ian Rabey's *The Back of Beyond* (1996). Currently, he is working on the dramatisation of Bulgakov's *Heart of a Dog*, commissioned by the Théâtre d'Esch, to be produced in 1998. He is also a writer of poetry and short stories. (Meyer-Dinkgräfe 2002, 271)

11 Antoinette Walsh trained at the Samuel Beckett Centre for Performance, Trinity College Dublin where she graduated with a BA (Hons) in Drama and Theatre Studies. She worked extensively as an actor in theatre, TV and radio in Ireland. Alongside her acting work she has 10 years experience as a tutor of improvisation, acting and voice and has taught at some of Ireland's leading drama schools including the Gaeity School of Acting, Dublin. Antoinette Walsh graduated with an MA Voice Studies from Central School of Speech and Drama in 2005. Since graduating she has taught as a visiting lecturer at RADA, London School of Dramatic Art and Central School of Speech and Drama, and is voice tutor at ASAD. She is currently investigating the relationship between voice and its architectural environment.
(http://www.cssd.ac.uk/staff.php/9/68/antoinette_walsh.html)

12 Gareth Potter, Welsh actor, see
http://www.cardiffcasting.co.uk/men/CVs/Gareth_Potter.htm

13 Roger Owen is a Lecturer in Drama at University of Wales Aberystwyth. After graduating from the University of Wales Aberystwyth Drama Department in 1987, he pursued a PhD in Welsh-language Theatre since the Second World War, while also working sporadically as a professional actor. Since finding gainful employment as a lecturer in 1994, he has continued to work in both an academic and practical capacity as a lecturer, actor/performer and director. His main area of teaching has been in Theatre and Performance Studies but he has also been known to conduct the odd Film seminar. Specific areas in which he has regularly taught include Performance Analysis, Performance in Context, Performance Writing, Theatre and Society and Analysis of Space. More sporadically, he has presented sessions on acting, directing, textual analysis, Shakespeare, 20thC English and American drama, and Welsh language theatre.
http://www.aber.ac.uk/tfts/staff/profiles/roo.html.

CHAPTER TWENTY-ONE

PERFORMANCE PRACTITIONER AND ACADEMIC: MIKE PEARSON

Mike Pearson[1] is Professor of Performance Studies at the University of Wales Aberystwyth. Interview with DMD, 16.1.2007

DMD
Following on from, and continuing a long and distinguished career as a performance artist/practitioner you now work as Professor of Performance Studies within a Department of Theatre, Film and Television Studies. How would you define "Performance" as the object of Performance Studies?

MP
This is a complex and interesting question. It presupposes that we are regarding *performance* as a particular genre or a particular kind of object of study. For me *Performance Studies* is in reality a set of approaches, or a kind of optic, for thinking about the broadest range of performance activities.

I have been involved in certain kinds of performance over the past 30 to 40 years that did however become an object of performance studies. This is related to the origins, the foundational moments of the discipline, with the work of Richard Schechner. Schechner comes from traditions of experimental and alternative theatre of the late 60s that first inspired me— I am of the next generation. Schechner's work with the Performance Group was important for me. As a young academic he began conversations with Victor Turner—Performance Studies itself emerges at that point, influenced by anthropology. The initial formulation is about setting contemporary performance in juxtaposition with other cultural and ethnological phenomena. At the base of the discipline then there are these particular practices emerging from the late 60s. What distinguishes all of them is that they are not reliant on the exposition of dramatic literature. They are formulated in and by other means. When I began work in the early 70s, I was very influenced by Grotowski, whose work had become increasingly known through the 60s; it was through the publication of *Towards a Poor Theatre* that he really entered theatrical consciousness. His proposal of a *poor theatre*, of taking apart the mechanics of theatre making and suggesting that those constituent elements might be in different ratios with each other or might indeed not be necessary all the time was extremely influential. Thus when I am talking about *performance* I am inevitably referencing certain kinds of genealogy.

If you ask me what performance means to me then, it is work and its exposition within which those ratios and combinations of elements that make meaning are different from, or an alternative to, the staging of dramatic literature. One might think about performance more usefully as something to do with manipulations of space, of time, of ordering of material, the use of different kinds of detail within that material, than one would find in the presentation of plays in the auditorium. That approach to ordering, in particular, is very significant; there may be no prejudgments about what material is more or less suitable for theatre. So it does not necessarily concern human motive, human story—it could equally well be a telephone directory or different kinds of data that find their way in. Increasingly now, those kinds of material might be ascribed to a whole variety of media within the mix of performance itself. Often there are not personages that might resemble characters, therefore ensuring coherence throughout the material, and neither is there necessarily narrative development, which would create a dramatic trajectory. Performance becomes like a piece of material that is in brackets, that is thus cut out from everyday life and that may have no resolution. Within it the performers may be increasingly asked to engage in discontinuous or interrupted kinds of activity. In one moment they may be engaging in a rhetorical engagement with the audience, in the next moment they may be doing nothing at all. Then they may be involved in a task-based work. In some work of the Wooster Group for instance, there are people on stage not engaged in dramatic activity, but who are still present. What is thus demanded of the performer is an alternative kind of practice that we are only just beginning to appreciate. It is not a distortion of dramatic acting; it requires other sorts of expertise.

Performance inevitably involves work with the body, work with space and place and for those very reasons performance studies is of necessity interdisciplinary. In the analysis and apprehension of performance we may need to appreciate other critiques - from gender politics to the latest formulations of place in geography. It may well be that what we do is also informing those approaches in other disciplines: there is an attraction of disciplinary interest towards us, and we are reflexively interested in those perceptions as well.

DMD
In the context of what you said so far, how would you see the relationship between performance and *play*?

MP
We should not forget that in the earliest attempt, by Schechner, to analyse performance in a different way, he suggests that there is a nexus of human activities: play, game, sport, certain kinds of ritual, and performance. They share characteristics: they are all, as purposeful activities, organised; there are implicit or explicit rules involved; they use time in different ways...many of these we also find in dramatic theatre. Within the nexus, these activities may fuse and interact—in fact they are so close together that you will see one in the other. I wonder whether we should be thinking more about rhetoric, and seeing these activities on a sliding scale, depending on the amount of rhetorical engagement and quotient in the exposition of each. I have long been interested in the presence of play in performance. My latest work is to some extent around children's play or children's perceptions of the world and it is helpful to think about that as present within the nexus.

DMD
Do you see yourself as a performance artist, as a performer? Do you have any preference for what you call yourself, or what others call you?

MP
There are endless questions of terminology. Every succeeding generation needs to stake its claim. I have a certain understanding of what *performance art* is. But then, performance art became *live art*, then it became *time based art*, today some university courses call it *time based practice*. Therefore, if you call me a performance artist, I am propelled back in time, as someone who practises performance art. I think *performance practitioner* is good enough.

DMD
You are both an academic and a performance artist. How did those two sides of your work *develop* in relation to each other?

MP

I became an academic teacher in 1997 at a moment in my professional career when I was full of questions and doubts. The one thing that I was keen to do was never to try to teach what I had been doing professionally, as a kind of genre. I was never convinced that the world in which an eighteen-year-old, or a nineteen-year-old lives, has any relation to the world in which I live. To try and sell this as a genre or a way of doing things did not seem to me to be very helpful. What I rather tried to do was to look at the practices I had been involved in over twenty-odd years and see whether there were emerging principles about the work that you could teach both theoretically and practically, as a kind of common sense.

One of the problems of performance is that there is no canon. There are pieces of work that we return to again and again, but that is more because they exist on video, they have a document. Certain works are reified, but I am not sure they are much more significant than a lot of performances that have simply disappeared. In Aberystwyth we do not have this incredible throughput of work that we can look at and refer to. Trying to work with principle and make what we can here was always my intention. Then there was the question of continuing to make professional practice and what the relationship is between those two. I am aware of trying to hold the two worlds apart. Definitely, when I work in the professional sphere, I do try to keep it professional. My work does not tend to arise from academic questions, but from artistic desire. Because I have no funding the work has tended to become rather conceptual—it cannot be ten people rehearsing for four weeks in a room. Working with Mike Brookes[2] it has become more about making plans, devising strategies that we then enact short-term.

DMD

This is then enforced by the outward conditions by independent of your academic existence?

MP

Absolutely, but actually rather reflective of the likely professional world that many of our students will enter into, because now the possibility of long-term funding has disappeared. Despite these conditions my professional work enables me to conceive work that we can consider academically.

DMD

And you then engage in an academic analysis of the project once it has been completed.

MP
Yes.

DMD
This is of course relevant in the current debate on the reflexive practitioner and the debate on *practice as research*.

MP
That is true certainly of the latest body of work, which is much concerned with dramaturgy and concept. Here it is rather easier to reflect on what is going on, with regard to structure and affect. I would have had much more difficulty some twenty years ago when I was a physical performer, engaging in that degree of (self-) reflection. You are quite right, though. I have been involved in debates on practice as research, but I have misgivings about the whole notion, largely because of this professional – academic interface and blurring, and because of this lack of canonical history. I very often see work, as a result, that is being enacted in academic situations that has professional parallels in the past. The problem of originality comes in here, of course. And within the academy performance has to be even-handed, has to come equipped with liberal credentials. In the professional context, you are making work to be provocative, to be extremely challenging. That's what makes great work what it is, that is why we want to see it.

DMD
Would you think that the academic aspect of analysis may interfere with the creative process, which you may want to locate at a non-intellectual, non-analytic sphere of your mind?

MP
In a way, yes. Making professional work often throws me back into contact with colleagues who have no interest in academic aspects and who would, indeed, be quite resistant to me if they thought I was wearing that hat whilst working. This is particularly the case with the German saxophonist Peter Brötzmann[3], the godfather of free jazz in Europe. It is always extremely enlightening to collaborate with him. It is not that he is anti-academic; it is just not on the palette, not on the table. Working with these free jazz players is very interesting: they only go with what you bring. If you cannot do it in the moment of doing it, it's no point being

there. Therefore, even if I do want to have some academic input I have to distil it into how I am present in that environment.

DMD
As far as I can see, much material in performance within an artistic context seems to be dwelling on the "dark" aspects of human life. I would place your production of *Angels*[4], some years ago in the Department, in that category. Is my generalisation appropriate? If so, could you think of reasons why there is this emphasis on the "dark" aspects, both in general and in relation to your own work?

MP
For me this has to do with my first interests and impulses in performance making. One of the earliest pieces of work that I did professionally was with two French directors on a series of texts by Artaud[5]. I did two solos, the first one entitled *Flesh*, based on some of his most desperate texts about the body physical. Artaud was always there in that initial thinking. I was subsequently involved in dynamic physical work, which led me to appreciate that certain things are revealed through the body *in extremis*. Recently I have become interested in classic performance art. I see great poignancy in some of those art works. Over the past three or four years I have hardly been to the theatre but I have seen a lot of performance art that frequently involves extremes of duration and extremes of duress, which are revealing in a way similar to long viewing or long meditation.

DMD
Duress, duration to transcend and suddenly reach a different, altered state of consciousness?

MP
Exactly. I think the great practitioners of that work achieve something truly revealing.

DMD
Would that altered state be achieved initially be the performer him or herself, and ideally transfer to the spectators?

MP
Yes. I am reminded more frequently these days of the old companies of the 1960s and early 70, because sadly more and more former colleagues are dying. There may have been misunderstandings involved, but I do

think that despite our very limited understanding we were aiming for certain kinds of cathartic response. Perhaps in our naiveté the only way we could imagine that was looking at what you call "the dark side"

DMD
What then are the criteria (if indeed there are any) of differentiating between experiments where this "works" and presentations that do not go beyond forms of narcissistic self-exhibition?

MP
Somehow we always manage to identify, as watchers, a degree of self-reflection. Thus even in very extreme work we are able to identify any fake element. Many experiences over the past years have informed that perception. My extensive work with severely disabled performer David Levett[6] was indicative of many things for me. An eminent theatre practitioner made the point to me that all we were ever looking at was his disability and that all the audience were doing were empathising with this man—one could never get beyond that stage of pity, he said. For me, that was simply not the case in David's work.

DMD
I remember seeing him once, at the Artaud conference organised by CPR in Aberystwyth; for me he was moving, and I did not feel pity but admiration for the way he managed his body not just for daily functions, which must be difficult enough, but for extra-daily performance.

MP
This is precisely the context in which the clash between fakery and authenticity becomes important. David could never make anything that looks like a conventional theatrical sign, very often because his body would say: "No way am I going to do that, at this point in time". Nevertheless, we appreciate him 'as signing', as expressing.

DMD
I had in mind, with my earlier question, the difference between, say, your production of *Angels*, which was very impressive as a performance (although I did not particularly like the effect it had on me), and the kind of engagement in violence that is no more than gratuitous.

MP
In the case of *Angels* there were certain crucial decisions that were made.

Perhaps they had to be made. They gradually began to inform how the work might develop. For example, I could not imagine any human way that one could bring that material to visual representation.

DMD
And so you set it in complete darkness.

MP
Yes. Also, it was a one-off situation—it was possible to work with that extraordinary group of young women. They wanted to do it when I suggested it. We are coming back to where we started this discussion: I am always pleased to think back to that work because, in an academic context, as a module for students, it was as good as I could conspire. In drama you have a text and you have traditions of interpretation and production that you can reference. For students of performance the question is always what do they have to go on: are they emulating distant professional practice and not bringing it off, or are they attempting something original within a specific context that might be difficult or impossible to present in the public sphere

Notes

1 Mike Pearson trained as an archaeologist. Between 1972 and 1997 - in a series of companies including RAT Theatre, Cardiff Laboratory Theatre and Brith Gof - he pioneered new and innovative approaches to the form, function and placement of performance in Wales and further afield - South America, Hong Kong, Eastern Europe... He currently works with Mike Brookes in the Pearson/Brookes company as well as creating solo performances. Mike joined the Department of Theatre, Film and Television Studies at the University of Wales Aberystwyth in 1997 and launched the Performance Studies degree scheme in 1999. In April 2002 Mike was Distinguished Visiting Scholar at the Centre for the Critical Analysis of Contemporary Culture at Rutgers, the State University of New Jersey, USA.
2 Mike Brookes is an artist and designer, working primarily as a painter and performance maker. His design work has engaged both graphic and time-based media; and his collaborations with performance companies such as Brith Gof, The Magdalena Project, Earthfall, and Quarantine, have resulted in a wide spread reputation for his activities as a lighting and production designer. See his website at http://www.mikebrookes.com/
3 Peter Brötzmann (b. 1941), German painter and free jazz saxophonist.
4 *Angels* was a production directed by Mike Pearson with students on the BA (Hons) Drama at the University of Wales Aberystwyth in 2002(?). The performance space was completely dark except for a strip of fluorescent light above the exit. The performers was in promenade style and began by performers

among the audience narrating medieval experiences of encounters with angels; the majority of the production's seventy minutes, though, consisted of excerpts, at times graphic details, from the court case of Fred West and his wife Rose, who together murdered twelve girls and women between 1967 to 1987. During the narrations performers moved among the audience, interacting with the spectators by physically touching them.

5 Antonin Artaud (1896-1948), French playwright, poet, actor and director,

6 David Levett is a musician and physical performer. He appeared with Mike Pearson in *In Black and White* (1992), in Brith Gof's productions *DOA* (1993), *Camlann* (1994) and *Arturius Rex* (1994), and in *Carrying Lyn* (2002).

PART IV:

LEGACIES

CHAPTER TWENTY-TWO

SHAKESPEARE'S LEGACY:
RICHARD EYRE

In 1980, Richard Eyre[1] directed Jonathan Pryce[2] as Hamlet at the Royal Court Theatre in London. In 1984, I asked him about his directorial approach for directing a classic at a theatre renowned for its focus on new dramatists.

Why *Hamlet*
Richard Eyre: I had been working then for about fifteen years in the theatre and I suppose for about fifteen years I had directed at least four plays a year, and a large number of classics, as well as contemporary plays which I had commissioned and seen through their finishing stages and directed, including works by Trevor Griffiths, David Hare and Howard Brenton. Max Stafford-Clark [who was the artistic director of the Royal Court, 1971-1993), asked me if I would do a play at the Royal Court, if I would do a classic there. And if you are asked to do a classic within that sort of context it has to be something that really resonates with contemporary meaning.

I suppose *Hamlet* was the play that I have long been attracted to, that I was attracted to and still am attracted to, as everybody is. It is difficult to escape the cliché, you know, that Hamlet is a mirror of our times.

The actual way that I came to want to do it was slightly curious. I was looking at—this was in 1980—I was looking at a picture, Dürer's *Melancholy*, a woman in a long dress sitting in a slumped posture, with an extremely weary expression, surrounded by all the scientific instruments of the Renaissance, and it was as if it was a metaphor for having arrived at a state of intellectual and scientific development and just being awed by the consequences and being wearied by the possibilities of choice. Anyway, I was looking at that and I was thinking: "Well, that's Hamlet, that's the sense in which Hamlet is the contemporary mind. And the eighties seemed to me to be absolutely an era where nuclear development came to a peak after protest for twenty years. In the eighties it really started to get serious, and we started to be faced with ecological problems. At the same time I was reading an essay by Günter Grass in which he said if I was to find an image of the eighties, if somebody asked me to quote an image of the 80s, I would say: Dürer's Melancholy. So I thought, well, that's some sort of synchronicity.

Anyway, I decided I wanted to do *Hamlet* because it seemed that I could make sense of it for that moment. An extraordinary thing about the play is that it does absorb the statements of the time. It is possible to look at a sixties Hamlet and a seventies Hamlet and an eighties Hamlet and see how they do act as a metaphor for the epoch. I suppose the fundamental thesis of the production was a kind of rationalist Hamlet. What I was trying to do was to make the play live for a contemporary audience, but without doing that kind of dislocation of changing the whole period, setting, costumes.

Contemporary appeal

I wanted to do it within an Elizabethan setting, within the Shakespearean period, but give it an absolutely contemporary appeal. This led me to various decisions. First of all, I wanted Jonathan Pryce to play Hamlet, who I worked with a lot before, he had been in my company in Nottingham, and we had done *Comedians* together, and many other plays together, and he seemed to me the quintessential actor of the eighties. He is kind of classless—he is from a working-class background, but I wouldn't say of Jonathan that he is of his essence a working class actor. I mean that's not the characteristic that comes across most of all. So I wanted him to play it.

From that decision radiated out various ways of playing it which coincided with the way I was looking at the play. Very early on I decided to cut the first scene of the play. It was a hugely unpopular decision, as you can imagine. This was because I had a very strong image of Nixon's inauguration, and I remembered that at the time he was being inaugurated it was just the time before the Watergate scandal was just bubbling up to the surface. In retrospect you looked at that inauguration and you thought: oh, the barefaced courage or foolhardiness of this man to stand up when this massive treachery was going on. I found it impossible to get away from this image at the beginning of the play which is why I started with the council chamber addressing the audience as if this was a state occasion. And I wanted to very strongly say that this is a bout real politics, that this really is, that power is important.

I wanted Claudius to address the audience in a rational way: you know, we had a lot of trouble, we had this death, we are all very sad about it, now we must go forward, and with his wife standing by his side, and presenting a public face, so he would immediately punch us as a very churlish man, this Hamlet sitting there and behaving badly in public.

And I wanted to make it perfectly clear that part of the tension, Hamlet's tension that was tearing him apart was the fact that he had to behave in public, he had to present a public face, and if he didn't, it was a very very radical act. So that to behave, to become, as it were, mad, was an act of revolution. I mean a subversive act.

Then the Ghost. I wanted to rationalise the play. I wanted to try and find an analogy for the experience of an Elizabethan audience, Shakespeare's audience, seeing the Ghost. At that time which was the late 16th century, there was massive scepticism about ghosts. Some people disagreed with me and said: oh, you don't understand that Elizabethan's believed in ghosts so you just cut it". It wasn't like that at all. What I was trying to do was to provide a contemporary equivalent of that sort of scepticism. Now today, we believe in demoniacal possession; you believe you have enough scepticism and you are credulous enough to believe this. Now it seemed to me that the key thing to dynamify Hamlet was: do I believe in ghosts or not? Is this true, or is this a figment of my imagination?

So it seemed to me you have to dramatise the dilemma. And I thought if you have a corporeal Ghost then the audience is immediately saying: "Oh, I know, this is this dramatic convention". So I thought we got to go for this, and because it was Jonathan, I mean Jonathan was an actor who could take it on board, and he could make it work, as probably very few actors in the world could; it had to be frightening physically, really disturbing, and it really disturbed him, you know, he just doesn't know what it happening to him: and that seemed to me the key point: he doesn't know whether he is mad or not. Simply that awful thing, doubting his own sanity, and that was the only way that I could make sense from scene to scene of the way in which his, and the public notion of his madness changes.

This, then, is the reason behind Hamlet's delay, procrastination. And also, he does have a sense of what a state is, and what is expected of a state. And it is very strongly, very strongly put over in the play in the role of Polonius. I think Polonius is an enormously powerful figure in that he ... he is a man who absolutely equates the personal conduct and public responsibility. They must be undistinguishable. So that his long speech to Laertes is precisely about all that. And he has spent a lifetime doing that to

Ophelia: You behave like this, you do this, you do that, he's not the one for you; everything is subjected to that kind of discipline. He is a man of state to the nth degree.

Another strategy I employed to make the production live for a contemporary audience is cutting incomprehensible passages, and I am quite unrepentant about it. I love the way the state, the responsibility of public man and of private man run parallel in the play. And of course once Hamlet commits murder he is tainted, It is no longer possible for him to maintain his identity, his balance. It seems to me that from that moment on he gets more and more nihilistic. When he comes back from England and this again seemed to me to be quite alarmingly true of our epoch, that he seems to be a man who, for Shakespeare's audience quite, quite shocking, who said there is no life after death, there is no God. He becomes death-obsessed; I mean he goes to the cemetery not because there was going to be a scene there; he goes there because he wants to face death. He says: well, what is it? It's nothing; there is nothing there—quintessence of dust—and he ends with "The rest is silence". This seemed to me an absolutely horrifying vision for a Shakespearean man that in the very moment he knows he is on the edge of the cliff—death—it's like the edge of an abyss, there is nothing there. I thus do not agree with opinions that Hamlet accepts providence and thus divine power to guide our destiny.

I cast a poet, Christopher Logue[3], as the Player King, and he rewrote the speech, because I wanted to draw attention to the fact that the language of the Player King is bad poetry. Yet, whenever I have seen it, it is kind of, well, it just sounded like more blank verse, and I just wanted to dramatise, push it further and say this is a very different language the player is speaking, this is highly dramatic, so that there would be a jarring effect. I never felt any kind of obligation to the text. I suppose I was keen to take a European attitude to the play. Not that I want to rewrite *Hamlet*, but that it seems to me you've got to make plays come alive. I am not ashamed of using any devices; of course, if they are gratuitous then they are defensible because they simply don't work. I don't see that there is a crime in substituting bad verse for bad verse.

The set was modelled on a room from a castle in Padua, a tabloid room. What we wanted was a sense of that Renaissance court where, quite literally, and metaphorically, the walls had ears, so that every way you looked you were never sure that you were alone. I mean it's like you can go to any Eastern European country. At first you think it's a joke, but when you are sitting here and they say, just a moment, and they go and switch on the TV, you get an insight into people living permanently like that. That is why I wanted to make very shocking that business of

Claudius and Polonius. I wanted that you never knew where people could come from. You never knew which was a door, so they could come from anywhere, and they go out through the wall and they're just hiding behind the wall. It's an awful thing; they are there the whole time listening to terribly intimate scenes.

I don't think Freudian labels are useful. I would say this is my biography for Gertrude. She was married young, very young, to a very austere autocrat, old Hamlet, who she worships and is somewhat in awe of. She is a good Catholic, a good church girl, and for whatever it is, 20-25 years, has lived an absolutely chaste life, marrying public and private life perfectly, in the shadow of a giant of a man, this real autocrat, old Hamlet. He was an extremely powerful fighter in the field, a powerful general, a military man, not an easy man to get on with. You know, it's substantiated, in the text. He dies, apparently perfectly healthy, he just dies. She's absolutely shattered, her life just drops apart. The brother is a waster, a drunk, and always in the shadow, and, I think rather younger than old Hamlet. He has for years, I always suspected, been making obscene propositions to her that she's been shocked by, and somehow, he awakens in her a sexual passion that hasn't been, probably never been awakened by old Hamlet. And she becomes like a young girl. Completely irresponsible.

And I wanted to try and show that she could not keep her hands off him. Not that she was a nymphomaniac; just she had never known that kind of passion of sexual love. Her son, whom she is terribly close to, and vice versa, is just appalled by this. My mother, whom I worshipped and had always thought of as a pure, wonderful and perfect woman, is behaving like a teenager, and kissing in public with this drunk, he just can't bear it. So I don't think there is anything more—it's more profound than that. It's a good working hypothesis. Not that they are unnaturally, sexually drawn to each other. I don't think he is. I think he has grown up as an only child, being treated as a prince always, set aside from other people, a single child, an intellectual, whereas his father is a man of action, with a mother who is never—who has never been particularly physically close to him. He is absolutely a product of that world, highly intelligent, highly sensitive, and he has never been able to immure himself to the necessary brutalities of politics. He has always kind of stayed above it. When his father dies he suddenly finds he's in the middle of it and he can't wash his hands of it.

Hamlet addresses the "to be or not to be" soliloquy to Ophelia. I wanted to do this because it seemed very strange in the play that he does the soliloquy and then he turns round. Where does she appear from? So I thought what would happen if she was there. We just tried it, at rehearsals. Jonathan just tried, he tried to speak to her, and it was the most extraordinary and powerful result. Because it is said to his only ally in the court, this young maid, saying: what to do, I'm so desperate. And she can't deal with him. She adores him, and he is very attracted to her. I wanted this scene to feel like a love scene, just on the edge of tremendous passion, of really strong affections. But of course the whole time she knows that she's being overheard, two inches behind her; she's absolutely terrified by that. She can't speak freely at all. And then there is the moment, and in fact I think that Jonathan made it very clear, where he is just about to say something to her that he hears something. He was almost physically sick, realising that she has betrayed him, yet another person, that she's just being used. That's what started him treating her just like "you whore, go, just get away. This what you want? Want to be treated like a whore; you're behaving like a whore. So I'll treat you like a whore"

Notes

1. Richard Eyre (b 1943). While artistic director at Nottingham Playhouse, he encouraged new writing by Trevor Griffiths, David Hare and Howard Brenton. In 1980 he was invited to direct a classic at the Royal Court, and chose *Hamlet*. Eyre's concept of making the classic come to life for a contemporary audience worked well, assisted by a virtuoso performance in the title role by Jonathan Pryce. Since 1980, he has also directed at the National Theatre, whose artistic director he was between 1988-97, succeeding Peter Hall. Productions there include the musical *Guys and Dolls* (1982), *Hamlet* (1989), Jonson's *Bartholomew Fair* (1988), *The Night of the Iguana* (Tennessee Williams, 1992), *Richard III* (1992, with Ian McKellen), *Macbeth* (1993), and a trilogy of plays by David Hare, *Racing Demon*, *Murmuring Judges*, and *The Absence of War* (1990-4). Under his leadership, the Royal National Theatre has been very successful commercially and artistically. (Meyer-Dinkgräfe 2002, 82)
2. Jonathan Pryce, b 1947, worked with the Royal Shakespeare Company in the 1970s, followed by a career in film and on television.
3. Christopher Logue (b. 1926) is a widely published poet.

CHAPTER TWENTY-THREE

BRECHT'S LEGACY:
HEINZ-UWE HAUS

Heinz-Uwe Haus[1] (b. 1942) in interview with DMD, November 2006

DMD
How did your interest in theatre first arise and then develop?

HUH
We were living in a small town on the outskirts of Berlin. In 1948 the film *The Bridge* was shot. I had blond, curly hair and blue eyes. They used many people from the town as actors for small parts. The director, Arthur Pohl[2], and some of the major actors lived at, or visited, our place. I remember Ilse Steppat[3], Steffie Spira[4], Arno Paulsen[5], and Karl Hellmer[6]. They used me again and again; I had to cross that bridge again and again. It was the only film that DEFA[7] shot in those years that dealt with the escape of refugees from the East and their arrival in a small town. After initial scepticism and rejection a major fire leads to cooperation between locals and displaced. Running across the bridge was the escape from the fire. The film was never again shown during the GDR years, it resurfaced only recently.

I think this was important, to some extent, because my memory of the filming and the actors never diminished. My mother was very young, Very early on I had two major desires: to study at university—at the age of fourteen I wanted to be a Romance scholar—and to be an actor. Later the desire to be a Romance scholar disappeared. I started theatre work when I was twelve years old. I worked with a group of other boys; we wrote little scenes and performed in a local pub. We documented most of our work, with photos. My grandmother supported our work, sewing the costumes. I tended to be the one in my form at school who always wanted to contribute something to public events, such as reciting a poem, or later putting together, as director and actor, sketches. In due course I thought that we needed to get adults involved. This led to writing sketches, in which adults participated, for example the wife of the town's Kriminalkommissar[8] who happened to live in our three-family house.

When I went on to high school, I joined the literary circle and I took over the school's amateur theatre company. My first work with that company was a Brecht evening—it was promptly forbidden triggered by its references to *Baal*. The accompanying programme notes were all spelt in lower case. The local people's library librarian had supported me in tracing relevant material, because Brecht had not yet arrived in the provinces. I felt that Brecht wanted to convey the immediate feeling that everything could be different—and should be so; that, when we see something happening, or shown in a story, it should surprise us. Suddenly we think: why is that so? One (permitted) question may lead to another question that is not permitted. I discovered that astonishment multiplies the possibilities of the course of history. Through Brecht I was able to reassure myself of the temporary nature of the existing order.

My main years of avid reading were when I was between fourteen and sixteen years old. I spent all my money on buying the collected works of Ibsen; I read Goethe, Schiller, Kleist, Benn, Rilke, Hebbel, Chamisso, Büchner, Nietzsche, Fichte, Freud, Strindberg, Hamsun, and all the Greek classics of drama that I could get my hands on. I tried to get hold of every book about painting I could. This was successful to a certain extent for the Renaissance to Menzel. Modern art was on the index, also all art that had been ostracised before as "decadent". Art postcards were handed around illegally. As far as Brecht is concerned, we tried to get everything in the text across very faithfully, for example, a specific haircut—for which I was, again promptly, reprimanded by a local party official when I spoke at a local event unrelated to my theatre activities.

DMD
The political dimension of your work is very clear in those early years already, with an emphasis on Brecht.

HUH
Yes, at a very early stage Brecht was confirmed, by representatives of the State, as having potential of resistance. What interested me in Brecht, in those days—and I still emphasise that this is what people should be interested in about Brecht—is the poet. After all, there are more poems by Brecht than lines of prose. What made me stay with Brecht was the reasonable and skilful way Brecht dealt with Marxist thinking and philosophy: it offered space.   The kind of political education, the

indoctrination, the doses of ideology, took place at such a primitive level, and the text books at school were written in such a mechanistic, dull way that my youthful instinct told me that all this was far removed from being remotely attractive, from being remotely true. We did know everyday reality! In this sense it was fascinating that Brecht offered a way of thinking that allowed space to think about it. Of course Brecht's seduction to cynical manipulation and his extreme lack of moral qualms became increasingly clear to me.

The daily reality of the regime was always juxtaposed with the experiences, truths and preconceptions of history, in general, and of my family in particular. In my case, for my Huguenot grandmother it was quite clear that she told me her prejudices about Catholics. My best friend at school, who is still a friend today, is a Catholic. If I know a little bit of history, all this is very clear. You grow up with these aspects of history and could thus consider all the things that happened in East Germany as a particularly crappy development of a post-war situation, without the possibility of questioning re-unification. All those phrases that we are the other, we are better, we are anti-fascists, this person is coming back, another one is coming back to us—from my perspective, then, this was not so interesting. Indoctrination was there, they tried hard, but people were not caught up by those phrases. In all of my school years I remember two form mates whom we classed as communist because their fathers were operatives. With them we were careful what we said—school in general taught first and foremost duplicity. Later we also found out that one of my classmates was working for the Stasi—he was not a communist, his parents weren't either, but they seduced him with his interest in technology, they offered him the opportunity of working with them on a jamming transmitter.

Later, when we moved to Berlin, there was a Swiss communist in the flat above, and he was a nice man. What I did not understand was how one could, as a Spain veteran, be a fatuous follower of Marxism-Leninism after so many years, and blandish the reality of the GDR. Wolfgang Heinz[9] was a trickster communist, the kind who tries to sell their dogmatism quite obtrusively, but then all is settled over a glass of wine. These people were also formed by their different life experience, and were thus able to see the talents of those who were not communists.

You must bear in mind that this was all very new to us. It was not so easy to draw conclusions, for that reason, and because of my age, then, anyway. I was the last one in my form to join the pioneers, and only because the teacher for whom I had developed much affection; I did it as a favour to her when once again I waited, early in the morning, in front of her house to share her way to school. For my generation all this did not mean much, yet. In our primary school form we had not a single child of communists. Later we had one such child, whom we considered as very exotic. Nobody talked to her, also because she spoke in very strong dialect—this was the time when Ulbricht[10] sent workers from Saxony further north so that they should become chair people of the LPGs. In my years in high school I sat next to a girl whose parents were West German communists. They would send their children to school here; her father was training to eventually take over a part of the city of Essen. She was very starry-eyed and believed in her parents' cause, but she returned to her parents in the West all the time. This was before the Berlin Wall. Other people would be busy indoctrinating you on a daily basis and then suddenly they had moved to the West. It seemed as though responsibility, moral judgment or solidarity did not play any role at all. If, from fear and suppression, everyday opportunism and amorality were to become the standard of behaviour, lived socialism would resemble past nationalism just too much. As a result, at the age of fourteen, the East did not have any interpretative sovereignty any more. I am happy that the same became true for my own son.

From early on in my childhood, I saw and sought to develop, theatre as a chosen niche to escape from reality. As a young man I was, naturally, animated by a transcendental ideal, not just by the desire to outlast the despised regime ducked away in hiding. At the same time I had the hope to serve the spectator, the colleague working with me, to give them strength by appealing to the possibility of change. It was clear to me from very early on in my life that the division of Germany was artificial. Fear of, and aversion against the regime led me to believe that theatre provided the space in which it was possible to resist the regime's attempts at educating us in conscious denial of inconsistencies. In my first year in high school, the teacher who ran our literature club—we read Rilke and George—gave me a copy of Nietzsche's *Zarathustra*. We had to write an essay and I quoted from *Zarathustra*. I was immediately summoned to the teacher's assembly to tell them who had given me that text. It was on the index, it was forbidden. The teacher who gave it to me was among the teachers who interrogated me.

DMD

After completing your secondary school education, you went on to train at the Filmhochschule.

HUH

I had to go into hospital for a year, to be in plaster bed for a bone condition, Scheuermann's disease. That year was a major burden for me; on my ward I was surrounded by people who were really ill, with congenital deformations. After that year I was allowed to return to school, quite normal, but I was excused from sports lessons; only at nighttimes I had to be in the plaster bed again. After I had completed high school I wanted to study at the Theaterhochschule Leipzig but they rejected me because I was not considered physically sufficiently fit. That theatre school would have trained me in the most conventional, worthy, or unsophisticated manner in Stanislavskian acting. So instead I was accepted at the Filmhochschule—strange, because that training involved much more physical work, including fencing and riding. They accepted my doctor's notes.

That was in 1961. The Filmhochschule was in the film suburb of Babelsberg. Immediately after the Wall had been built, we were working in a building close to the Wall; day in and day out we were confronted with the Wall, with the dogs, and the dog kennels, just across the narrow road. In the mornings the GDR border patrol would occasionally poke around in the waterway by the border with long sticks and drag bodies ashore, of people who had drowned while trying to escape. They dumped huge amounts of barbed wire into that water. We saw all that brutality, but my world-view did not develop further as a result, it had already fully formed. I had been confronted, at an early age and for a long time, with post-war conditions and had always been keen to see this part of history completed in a humane fashion, which in turn had fostered my ability to critique existing conditions. I did not accept Adenauer's view that freedom as he described it should only apply to the three Western sectors of Germany. I am aware that as a child or an adolescent you make mistakes in your judgment, but I preferred the nationalistic rhetoric of Schumacher. In addition, in those days the GDR tried, not as explicitly as later, to present itself as the better Germany, with reference to German national heritage, and in the name of unification of Germany. For about twenty years they spent time dividing West Germany into units of administration and to train the party cadres for West Germany. A dramaturg I worked with later on in my career already held his job for Frankfurt/Main, for which he trained, for years, to take over one part of that city. Much of German heritage from before World War I was blacklisted in that process of playing with eventualities, or re-interpreted to match the idea that socialism was the natural peak of all the developments of those years.

One of the reasons they had accepted me for the Filmhochschule was that I was not the conventional beauty. The selection of girls was predominantly for looks. The training was geared towards Stanislavski, but in my case I was strongly influenced by a voice and speaking instructor who had been working already before the Nazi regime; she was originally from Leipzig. The leader of Filmhochschule's acting department was also an actor, one of the old school who was still formed to the extent that post-war Moscow Stanislavski could not confuse him. We also had the translator of Stanislavski as a permanent acting teacher. From him I learnt about Stanislavski's ethics, especially the importance of learning in a context of discipline, and learning to serve the art. This teacher demonstrated in his own daily work what Stanislavski was talking about. He showed us what kind of place the stage is, how to deal with one's costumes, all those things that make the profession important and valuable and that enable the development of the actor's self esteem. He gave us the vital insight that the actor's expressions on stage are not only the actor's own business, but that they need to be regarded in context. In addition to my training I also studied film dramaturgy.

DMD
After completing your training you were sent into employment at the theatre in Senftenberg as an actor. What was that first professional employment like?

HUH
The theatre in Senftenberg was meant to provide entertainment for the workers in the local coal mines. It was a major culture shock for me. We had to sign a two-year contract, all workplaces were socially secure. After only three months I knew for certain that I had to get out of there at all costs, because I would not have been able to endure two years. That was not in line with the state intentions for work. It was not a question of the theatre itself. There were wonderful colleagues and I learnt a lot, how to work with texts. It was a question of the social conditions. The coal dust in the town was such that a new shirt was black with dirt by lunchtime. But I couldn't take it off because there was no chance to wash myself. I didn't have a water pipe in my accommodation, the toilet was across the courtyard, and I had to get water in a bowl. The theatre operated a touring system, where the places we toured to were at times so far way and even worse: in one place the bed was placed on slatted frames because the ground water came up to the floor level.

Already at that stage I was interested in directing for the theatre and sought to get work as an assistant director. I got that work; it was on a production of Shakespeare's *Romeo and Juliet*. And that was a culture shock as well. I had been used to directing in amateur contexts, but here, in the professional context, my role as assistant director was reduced to a kind of serving that I did not like. I was happy and willing to serve Goethe, and Schiller and the technicians, I could serve the development of a production, but I was not happy with having to serve the narrow-minded power games of such a small theatre apparatus.

I managed to get away after one year. The Filmhochschule had intended for me to go to the Filmhochschule in Moscow, which would of course have been the most desirable honour for most artists of the world. I could not have imagined anything worse than having to set foot in Russia. This offer allowed me to resign from my contract with the theatre in Senftenberg. Instead of going to Moscow, however, I joined the Stadttheater Brandenburg for a very enjoyable time. Here I enjoyed everything a provincial theatre can offer. The stage was not too large, I played a good range of different parts, the townspeople loved their theatre, the actors were local stars who were treated preferentially at the local butchers or bakers; my landlady had rented out to the theatre for many years. I was not too far away from Berlin, and we did not tour.

Here I had my first opportunity of directing, a Christmas fairy tale, *Frau Holle*, based on Brothers Grimm. On the side I directed some work elsewhere and organised recitations of literature, also for the "club of intelligence". This club existed in those GDR times: party authorities wanted to draw in the intelligentsia of the town, so as to be able to observe them, eavesdrop on them and thus control them. We did not know about all this at the time, though.

DMD
From Brandenburg you managed to return to Berlin, soon joining the Deutsches Theater.

HUH
I had hoped that the dramaturg of Besson[11], who had been one of my teachers, and who had seen me in number of productions, would see to it that I move on to Besson's company. Instead, they wanted me as Besson's assistant, as a master disciple. At the same time I had an offer from the Volksbühne to join them as an assistant. This was not so much on the basis of the directing work I had done already. It came about perhaps through the interest that Besson had in having me work with him. I decided to join

Besson at the Deutsches Theater. When I joined Besson, with my position as Meisterschüler, which was funded under the auspices of the Akademie der Künste, for the duration of three years, Besson had to leave; he had to move from the Deutsches Theater to the Volksbühne. My position now was that I was at the Deutsches Theater, with my Meisterschüler position, but without a Meister (master). In this situation it was helpful that I knew the Intendant, Wolfgang Heinz, from two assistantships with him (among other with *Hamlet*) during my years as a student.

DMD

You had first direct encounters with the regime, especially the state security services (Stasi) in Brandenburg already, and you mentioned your very early awareness of the political situation you grew up in. At the Deutsches Theater, you became the youngest fully contracted director in the history of that theatre. Tell me about the working conditions there.

HUH

I got the invitation from Berlin to become first assistant to Wekwerth[12]. I accepted. Wekwerth had been ill and did not return to the BE; he founded a working group at the Deutsches Theater. He really wanted to found an alternative BE, to eventually take over the existing BE. This determined my path in life for many years to come. I became the youngest director ever to work with the Deutsches Theater. It was also a time of political pressure. I had started a night program at the DT; before this, there was no theatre in East Berlin that started later than 8 pm, apart from late night Jazz performances. I did a Tucholsky evening, for example, or an evening of poetry and scenes—all in all a new form of literary revue. It was very successful indeed. It became successful, among other things, because we, for example, managed to have 150 roses thrown into the auditorium every night. They were quite difficult to get hold of in East Berlin. I also had a music group, which became quite influential later, with Günter Fischer. It was the first time that jazz or pop musicians worked with theatre. Conservative voices came up already then, whether such work was suitable on the stage of the DT. Another evening was with Stanislav Lem, the Polish science fiction writer. Then, in 1970, I got the major request to put together a great revue, together with a TV program to be based on it, which I was asked to direct as well. The DT got a new Intendant in the meantime, Hans-Anselm Perten[13], a strict SED party follower from Rostock—before he developed his career in the GDR, he was a member of the propaganda department of the imperial broadcasting under the Nazis. He held a special status with the party, and as a result he was allowed, occasionally, to put productions of West German authors on the DT stage. However, his appointment to the DT meant that political pressure at the theatre increased considerably. Up to that point you were secure, to a large extent, under a charming Vienna communist like Heinz. Perten wanted to demonstrate his power, and censorship was rife. The revue opened to critical acclaim, but it had been reduced by some thirty-five minutes of rehearsed material. It became worse for me when Perten was replaced by Gerhard Wolfram[14], who came from Halle. Behind the mask of obligingness he took the next opportunity—a revue of soviet texts "Better to have a crane in the sky than a tit in the hand", to tighten the thumbscrews and ended my career with the DT.

DMD
After you had left the DT Wekwerth invited you to join the Regieinstitut. Your theatre work and your political thinking reflect your position as a theatre artist within the totalitarian regime. Not much is known about such everyday-life conditions.

HUH
I learnt much from Wekwerth and I valued him as an artist. Although I know today about his role in the Stasi, I experienced him as more of an agent of security than the opposite. This is a bending of facts, just as it is known from prisoners who do not want to reproach their kidnappers. Wekwerth was no stirrer; he was an appeaser. It is quite clear that through him the Stasi was able to comply with its operative concerns and that at the same time the regime did not suffer any damage. When I did things that were against the expected norms of behaviour, for example while travelling to the US, I was punished. Wekwerth did not do anything against that, of course, but the punishment was meaningless, I remained the representative of him, the artistic director. Brecht's master disciple at least had his goal before his eyes. Perhaps, however, in some instances the teacher of mathematics and physics came through, which he had been before he moved to the BE.

For this regime there is, at no corner or any phase of my heart, only the slightest justification or excuse. All the big talk about the anti-fascist movement—all those people were strict followers of the SED. But what about the majority of the population, who had problems not only with the way politics was made, but also with the very justification with the existence of the regime. They weren't all Nazis. Whatever antifascism we had, we achieved painstakingly and independent of the fascistic regime. The horrors of war formed my generation. Its senselessness as well as its crimes became clear to us through its consequences. My father was spotter in the Luftwaffe, Shortly before my birth my mother receive the notification that he was missing in action. He had not returned from a flight in the Caucasus. We had to think through ourselves what our soldiers did and how terrible the displacement was. But these were not the stories we heard: when the Russians came, they arrested the social democrats, not just Nazis. Whoever had a halfway functional capacity of judgment could only keep their distance from collaboration with the communists and to the Russian occupation power. My substantial distance to the protestant church came about despite my initial aim as far as profession was concerned: I wanted to become church leader. As a small child I saw Niemöller[15] and admired him. I also admired a soldier's virtues, which I knew from literature. I then learnt, again and again, how this regime was not mine, that there was no space there for me. The protestant church in due course began to align itself with the regime.

This natural belief that the GDR regime was only a temporary state of affairs was characteristic for many people of my generation, born in the early 1940s. We experienced the attempted escape, we all wanted to get to the American zone. The SS people gave me shelter, when I was three years old, while the Russians were not very nice to me—they took my bike away from me—they couldn't ride it properly, tried to use it as a scooter and it broke. Then my mother and relatives told me all the things that happened while escaping—why did all the women have to hide in the cellars. I heard all those things as a small child. I collected all those contradictions and that's why we hate these contradictions so much. Against that background I could never believe that it was God's will that the Soviet-occupied zone should develop into the alternative Germany and that the other three zones should hurry to join it. When I got older I was of course able to realise that all the later distortions about the cold war and socialist world union were only politics of the day, because they kept changing from one SED plenary meeting to the next. You also noticed that a book that was referred to in one plenary was forbidden by the next one. The fact alone that you are not allowed to read something. Why? As far as TV was concerned, I saw GDR TV only occasionally, when I had participated in the program. I started reading *Neues Deutschland* from the age of twelve, and so did my son. We read together, and then discussed what we read, and both he and I were able quite early on to read between the lines, what had been left out.

If someone was aware of the situation he lived in, here, and if he wanted to get along with himself, he was able to see through the regime. Three times in my years in Brandenburg, and twice in Berlin I was set upon to become a member of the party, to further by career. Always, interestingly, after problematic events. I always managed to argue very philosophically and abstractly, saying that I'm no good at discipline, and using the problematic events as confirmation. Maybe I was just lucky with the people whose task was to get me into the party. One of them is today the principal of Ernst Busch Hochschule in Berlin.

Just for fun, after the fall of the Wall I reclaimed my former post at the Regieinstitut. We had been made part of the Ernst Busch Hochschule in Berlin, after having been independent and only nominally affiliated to the Filmhochschule. The panel set up to evaluate my application to get my post back was made up of four people. Four from the former East Germany, and the chairperson from the former West Germany. The colleagues from the former GDR included the person who holds the post now; he is the person who had, in a different context, initiated politically motivated disciplinary proceedings against me, had made sure that I had my permission to teach at university level withdrawn and had me banned from any contact with students for a year. The Stasi was only *one* of the party's means of suppression. When we talk about the Stasi today, we must not ignore their employers. As if in mockery I was later invited to attend his 65th birthday celebrations. Later I applied for a professorship in acting, but only former party members were even considered for the shortlist. Only now some people from the West are in there. These events confirm, how enduringly disastrous the training, for years, of many West German intellectuals to conjure away from their horizon terror and misanthropy, has burdened since the revolution in autumn 1989 the process of reunification.

In comparison, this school was more open in GDR times, because you had to integrate all these contradictions artistically. Nobody knew of the others how devoted they were to the party. In 1990 it seemed to me that all they had in common was their past in relation to the party. In that past, artists would be aware of their political differences, but never overtly: we always worked on a very professional level. My political problems related to being associated with Brecht came because the average party politicians did not at all understand what Brecht was all about—their cultural horizons ended with operetta. In this context I must go back to Wekwerth: his arrogance and his way of working were in a way quite Richard III-like, his intellectuality and his methods, sitting down and writing letters to some of these central committee people. Nobody else dared. Wekwerth, however, believed that he could do this because of what he, Wekwerth, represented as an artist. All this was accepted, somehow, within the political framework of the BE. When I had my first request to do work in the USA denied, I asked the Greek trade attaché to bring me, from West Berlin, as much literature as possible. I happened to know him because he was a native Cypriot, I had met him in Cyprus when I directed a production there. He would park his car three roads away from my place and come over disguised as a gardener or something like that. The American cultural attaché as well, he came over with a camera and some money.

The use of Brecht as a weapon for survival was what formed me right from the beginning. Learning from and working with Wekwerth and working in the institute even under observation by the Stasi became possible only with Brecht—no other system of thinking or argument would have assisted as much to help saving one's neck, again and again. Day-to-day life had other sides to it as well, also under GDR conditions: if a production was successful, some people breathed a sigh of relief that a production was a little bit different, a little more refreshing that what was otherwise on offer.

Wekwerth and his kind of colleagues, who considered themselves, within the system of the GDR, as the critical forces of the system, would even have been satisfied if people had developed a certain artistic way of dealing with the regime which would have allowed them top secretly create their free spaces. One day our party secretary had the nasty idea of introducing a new subject: political behaviour, allowing directors to both sell their work better and also to serve as a safety measure for themselves. We all tended to read the occasional book that was not available in the state library. As far as the party elite was concerned, there was a group of SED members who thought they could be so clever as to provide the awkward, brutal party machine with more sophisticated tools, a kind of humane inquisition. As long as things were not directly expressed they were tolerated in the 1980s. The times of the 11th SED Plenary, where they ideologically discussed the acceptable colour mocha cups (black mocha cups were considered inappropriate by some), were over. What was essential then was for the regime to cling on to power—they had realised that quite clearly. In addition, they tried to people to grab hold of the majority of the population that had nothing to do with the regime. Those who worked as grabbers was allowed (to use a metaphor from the Nazi regime) to be a Jew.

DMD
As I said before, much of what you tell me about conditions of working in the theatre in the GDR are not known to many people today.

HUH

The implemented terror of socialism found powerfully eloquent apologists in the free world. How else could I take Ernst Bloch's *Principle Hope* seriously, when he philosophises that in the Soviet Union Christ had for the first time come to power as Emperor; what perversion of his intelligence that he redefines the Moscow court cases as pacemakers for a more beautiful future. What is to be thought of Georg Lucacs, who, too, justifies the red terror as bridging towards a non-violent future? Neruda, Rolland, Aragon, Shaw and so on—the prostitution of philosophers and poets of the 20th century makes you nauseous. And nobody can make excuses with regard to ignorance that allegedly reduced their guilt. In *Archipel Gulag* (p. 172, Munich, 1974), Alexander Solschenizyn provides the simple answer: "Ideology. It is this that provides the evil deed with the sought-for justification, and the evil-doer with the necessary hardness. That social theory helps him to whitewash his deeds before himself and others, not to hear reproaches, not oaths but homage and praise".

DMD

You are well known as a director and exponent of Brecht. Brecht is commonly set up against Stanislavski. How do you see their relationship?

HUH

Brecht and Stanislavski have hardly anything to do with each other. Brecht was a great director, Stanislavski is not a director. Brecht was a great dramatist, Stanislavski was not a dramatist. Stanislavski was a teacher of acting, which Brecht never was. Stanislavski came from a tradition of theatre he wanted to maintain and develop further, while Brecht endeavoured to break traditions. Stanislavski found dialectics physically repulsive, to judge from photos of that gentleman, while Brecht was all but a gentleman and dialectics turned him on particularly. You could carry on with this list to avoid this mechanistic alleged antagonism. There is no point setting them against each other. They are talking about different things, although at some stage Brecht, under pressure from the formalism debate, under the pressure from attacks his theatre was subjected to, gave a list of fourteen things he had in common with Stanislavski.

The discussion of realism, which is at the centre of the alleged conflict between Stanislavski and Brecht, was about which difficulties of writing the truth we were responsible for ourselves. The truth, in this context, had to concur with an ideological grid—a permanent attempt at rape. That is why, interestingly, no technique, no concept of theatre that made its way onto the stage in the revolutionary 20th century, was better suited than

Stanislavski's. I immediately noticed that all the others had been killed, literally, and only Stanislavski existed on. Stalin had his reasons for keeping Stanislavski. He was the least problematic. All the books bout directing that Stanislavski's disciples wrote about the work of their teacher deal with dreadful productions within an agenda of propaganda. Thus the method must have had aspects to it that allowed it to be put to the regime's service. What was this? For me it became clear quite early that it contains an element of lie. Even in my own training at the Filmhochschule, which I value much, I wanted to approach reality or truth in the same way as the graph approaches the asymptote, never quite. We had to work with onions, backstage, so as to be able to cry in the appropriate moment. Of course we were carried away by the momentum of any feeling without knowing what we were saying. All these errors in the system that I noted as a student of acting, the somewhat sultry atmosphere of some rehearsals. Almost every student trained with Stanislavski has experienced, at least once, that enormous dependence that was allowed to develop between teacher and student. This has to do with the Stanislavski being a system of justification. It justifies the action in an inward direction. It organises feelings from within an extremely limited range of experience. It completely excludes the telling of stories. This does not mean that you can be anecdotal. If you re a genius there is no harm. If you have a speech impediment and you get a good speech teacher, the system works as well. Where it finds its limitation it becomes tangible, usable, for a totalitarian regime. It is like glycerine for the tears of a film actress for the justification of behaviour. Reading a ply such as to understand the sequence of scenes as one scene developing from the preceding one misleads to assume an immanence of the characters. As spectator you thus attend an event that does not invite you to interfere with your own feelings and your own contradictions. This does not allow play with the audience but enables concrete audience isolation. All these are interesting endeavours, but to me they revealed a certain lack of responsibility that I was led into as an actor.

Hardly anyone can read a play properly. What does reading mean? It means understanding, but not intellectual understanding or re-cognition of knowledge or thought or larger contexts. It is, rather, the ability to suddenly rediscover, and to see gain changed, and to enter a relationship with, the unexpected, the strange aspects of a text, of events, from within a rich treasure of stories you have in your head, of observations you have in your head. When I have to stand on the stage as an actor, I have to be taught that there is an audience out there, say four hundred people, with four hundred stories. Before I even open my mouth these people know what they want to hear. Even if they don't know the play, if they have never heard of it before. That's the reality of the theatre: people come in with they stories and want to see that story and none other—and then they see *Faust*. Three of them may know something—a character from the Middle Ages; Marlowe wrote a play about him. But that does not make it easier for them, because they see their story only in a more specific context. People will only accept anything beyond what they came to see if I tell them such strange, unexpected, contradictory stories, which invite them to weave their own stories further, to give them up, change them. While I trained as an actor I felt that such a process is quite difficult to achieve with Stanislavski.

I found something else difficult. Although many of the productions Stanislavski talks about are socialist plays, or had social contexts, it all emerged from the head. You had an image of the character and tried to execute that image, to expand on it, to mould it, to portray it, to fill it with clarity, to transfer it. That is a tendency that goes against telling stories because it is within the spectator that this image of this character, this human being, this very special Borkman develops. As an actor I rather have to learn to be exposed to situations where I encounter social contradictions, social features, and unexpected combinations. Training needs to enable actors to do this—it should not just be done by the director. To invent such stories we need socially alert actors who observe in reality that human being slaps his daughter in the face and the next moment gives her a sweet. This is not interesting on its own, as a pathological case, on stage—it is not a state that is a biological given: it has social causes and does not exist without contexts. You must be able to relate to such contexts. Stanislavski could not possibly have developed, in his Soviet Union context, this way of developing emotional memory on the basis of stories with social contradictions. It is not surprising that Soviet Stanislavski, which means Stanislavski with certain emphases, became so popular in the GDR. His technique was meant to justify the artificial working class heroes, the artificial Soviet heroes, these characters that emerge from the head, from abstraction, from ideology. A training that was geared towards openness, towards telling stories, towards a canon of forms, does not do all this. Stanislavski is against montage, Brecht used this all the time. In the years of my training these were the kinds of experiences where on the one hand I relished the opportunity of not being responsible for anything, of being able to withdraw, of being able to madly traipse round in the limelight, to be only with myself and to give myself up and to sell all this as art. This is always an actor's primordial drive, to be exhibitionist and irresponsible, that's what the ramp is there for. In those days I didn't know yet what a peep show is, but classical Stanislavski productions are peep shows that you attend. The entire demeanour of Brecht's approach without ramp, also Shakespeare's approach without ramp. Demand different techniques. A Shakespearean *aside* is not a psychologically suspect stammering into one's shirt sleeve. Rather, it represents a level in which elements of the entertainer, of the jester and joker are part of the picture. If I accept this, I have an opportunity to playfully, with the audience, engage the audience with my and with their story. I engage them in a table tennis match, but for that I need the qualities of a good entertainer, such as Johnnie Carson[16] or Harald Juhnke[17] to have an eye on the audience—I have an eye on them even if I am being sarcastic.

I don't consider myself a guru in the same sense that many of the US Strasberg imitators portray themselves. On the whole, they have not been able to be open to the material they identify themselves with. Such openness requires a different way of thinking. Stanislavski's techniques are all very private; you cannot say anything against them as such because they are so private that they are of no significance when the play is about something different. This always interested me: theatre as an institution in society, theatre as orchestra. Thespis: the event that consists in one person getting up and stepping in front of a group. My early enthusiasm for Niemöller as church president was in relation to the role of the sermon— the correct and different sermon. The singsong of actor Moissi's[18] way of speaking on stage has the power of Walt Whitman. This kind of power is like a blade of grass that is able to penetrate concrete, in people's heads. A clown, a comedian, has the same power. All the things that come from that direction, though, from where genuine theatre is located, are beyond anything Stanislavski could ever hope to offer. That's why I have always maintained the greatest of admiration for the genuine comedian. Also in the run-down sense, because theatre belongs where people make their decisions or where they give themselves over to a moment of illusion of creating their own social spaces. That is on the fairs, at carnivals, the use of masks, Commedia del' Arte, that Neuber woman, the English players who travelled through Germany, all these were traditions beyond Stanislavski.

When I studied *Hamlet* as the last scenic studies at the Filmhochschule, I was able to apply Brechtian analysis to the text, to arrive at sub-scenes and to try out attitudes in those sub-scenes which I put together in a montage. It may have been a very mechanical process, with one not matching the other. I wanted to understand that behaviour consists of jumps and not of transitions. I wanted to find out that you tell one thing after the other—that a character does not have to be definable in scene one. A character comes into existence only by being different in scene one and in the last scene. And in between umpteen times different, so that I as an actor organise "confusion" for the spectator so that he keeps being surprised at all the things this character does. I have to discover that in the first place. That's what the characters of the classic period are like. They are not dry substrates from a thousand cases, but one case in all its possibilities. The possibilities are in the heads of those who study the case, who read the case, in the stories that the spectators have in their heads. I realised that because I had numerous stories in my head that I was unable to tell.

Without doubt, under the conditions of the SED dictatorship (as during the Nazi regime), the mutual attentiveness between stage and audience was more intensive and more explosive (because something was at stake) than in the liberal West German democracy. Independent of the schools from which the actors came, when the moment was right the audience determined what they saw. It challenged to see specific things. For that reason there was always a dialogue with the audience. This applies only to the performances that did not make use of ideology through the Stanislavski system. If there was reference to telling stories, even hidden stories, this was done through the principle of using collage in constructing a character. If text was maintained in contradiction to action, if text and action were contradictory, we know from the classics that this is often the case. We can notice with Tellheim[19] and all interesting characters that it gets interesting only if a contradiction can be detected. You therefore have to look out for such contradictions. A time of such contests as during my training as an actor enabled me to accept seriously only a technique that allowed me to work covertly and to realise the values of language, of poetry, of rhythm and verse, as elements of narration. I am concerned that most followers of Stanislavski—schools, teachers—are not bothered with the issue of telling stories. Instead, I realise that through outward signs they are trying to tell us their ideological positions. This brings us straight back to where Stanislavski could be abused very easily, used, utilised, to pump up any actor into the Government Inspector[20] while outwardly creating a caricature of the associated social system. It's not that Stanislavski did not demand the study of social conditions. He did that right from the beginning, only through this could he, like Georg von Meiningen[21], support realistic detail. That's not the point. He remained stuck, as I see it, in a view of the art of acting that was imminent in theatre itself. His methodology emerged from the art itself. This made him vulnerable later on: the rhetorical, empty cartridges he had at his disposal as an actor made for brilliant literary recitations led to an awareness that he was able to make the things more humane and natural. Storytelling is about something different, though. It is not about whether people are natural. It is about that nothing is natural if it turns into a public question. That makes the process social.

When dealing with Brecht, don't be discouraged, because initially those people were dealing with Brecht who got it wrong. They tended to be happy because Brecht presents poverty as something unnatural. This was an ideological treatment in the same way that Stanislavski was treated ideologically. As a result, the West discovered man Brecht-techniques—there is in fact nothing like a Brecht method. The dramatist Brecht, who was a great stage director, gave indications how to deal with a dramatic text in a responsible manner if you are pragmatic. It is something completely different that Brecht develops a way of thinking in which he does not ask "what kind of technique do you have?", but "what kind of contradictions are you interested in, that should make their way on to the stage? Can you see this contradiction in the form of slapstick, or in the form of an aria"? And so he brought both the slapstick and the aria to a production.

The author Brecht referred the three versions of *Galileo* each to the relevant social conditions at the time of writing—fascism, Hiroshima, cold war. In the cold war context, he had to write a play under conditions where it was difficult for him to show his colours—so he wrote about Galileo's difficulties of showing his colours. With few dramaturgical changes he told a different story each time. This was to do with changes in society, but how he told those stories had to do with the respective actors he worked with. There are descriptions of his rehearsal work, which demonstrate how both actors claim, and contribute, what constitutes the aesthetics of these solutions. Brecht as dramatist accepted his plays as plays only after their first production. The actor's dramaturgical action is what is special to Brecht. It results from a different kind of thinking and understanding of the actor's role in the production process. It is the responsibility towards the public.

Brecht's ensemble was quite a mix of people, some actors came from a boulevard context, some from municipal theatres, some had their political past, some had been in the resistance, people with vastly different social homes, who were eager to develop the ways they knew, understood and related to other people, and equally eagerly underwent these procedures. They sensed that here was someone—Brecht—who was thinking in a different way. Or they knew, or they were co-workers, or ideological conspirators. That's why it did not matter as much who played which parts. In comparison with the state theatre, the Deutsches Theater, with the German municipal theatres, where it was known who would play the heroes and who were the character actors, the BE was rather a panopticon—because in life, too, people never look and are as you expect them to be. The imagination that a king—this is a social story—can do what he likes, is wrong. How often, though, do we hear in rehearsals at municipal theatres: "But I'm a king, I can do that". But he cannot! Whether I get to power as dictator, as Kim Il Sung, as Margaret Thatcher, as Bush, or Mrs. Merkel—as soon as I have come to power, through elections, through bloody upheaval, because the predecessor has left office, the people, the audience, expect an inaugural celebration of some kind, a speech. That's how it has been for all times, there is no change here. These issues are political. The politics is that Gorbatchov assuming power does not differ from Hitler assuming power. That of Margaret Thatcher is not different from that of Richard III. Every example has a drawback—in this case there is one difference: Richard forgets it. That's his first sentence. He makes this one big mistake and that causes his eventual fall. That's why he loses the approval of the audience, and of Buckinhgam. They all expect a coronation and he does not comply with that expectation. After that he has hardly any asides any more. After that he believes in his position as given by Grace of God. From then on it's no longer Richard III, whom we all love, because he is no more bloodthirsty than all the other characters he has to deal with. Up to that point he's not (perceived to be) that bad after all—he is the first to introduce a constitution, before others even thought of a constitution. He was the first to act in a more democratic manner. That's where he makes his mistake. We notice these things, as a people.

The amazing parade on the occasion of the GDR's 40th anniversary, with people calling out Gorbachov's name. All the old guard, led by Honecker[22], were standing there, pale as chalk. You could see from the pictures that this was a turning point. They had miscalculated. These political issues are also issues of narration; as a director, but also as an actor I have sense them, I have to be interested in them when I do a play. I have to wonder. I can't make something out of everything that I wonder at. It has to be a fundamental attitude, a fundamental methodological approach to reading plays.

In contrast to Stanislavski I always try to counter the private element. All those procedures are the most simple, especially for a young person, enforcing and confirming how important all their private problems are for the stage—they may have got pimples, a psychosis, greasy hair, may have problems with the girls or with the boys, we can make all these work for the theatre. All this, in my opinion, does not have anything to do with theatre, all this belongs to therapy. We are going on stage, as actors, because of some hidden egomania. But then theatre offers us the opportunity to serve, entirely unselfishly and selflessly. To serve poetry, to serve the unfathomable, the miracle. For that we have to develop skills, from tap-dancing to beating the drum, from *Kleiner Hai* all the way to a new *Großer Hai*. That has nothing to do with how I organise feelings so that I get understood most comprehensibly. I remember how I cried when I saw *Mother Courage* as a young man. Rightly so, and my tears came at the right moment, when Katrin is shot. Of course it hurts to see when Mother Courage shares responsibility in her son's death, through her haggling, because she does not ransom him. Of course you people don't want to see that. Of course people don't want to see how crippled they are. But it is the actor who is capable to impact on this sore point of a human being—because in the very next moment we see how shaken this woman is. Weigel created the silent scream for her, for which Brecht was inspired by an image of a screaming Japanese woman at Hiroshima. What's wrong with Weigel imitating that Japanese woman's scream? The impact, that for me my crying gets stuck in my throat and that I notice a similarity with one, or two, or many situation(s) that I was in myself. After World War II, the people who had fled from their homes, who now sat in the cold, unheated theatre, of course they did not want to see this, they would have preferred to see operetta—let's forget the time for two hours.

In those days, Brecht wanted, just as you push the dog with its nose into its poop, to remind people of something they didn't want to hear. This is part of the method, to a certain degree, to use hot and cold to keep people always awake, because always there is the potential of reading the story differently. There is always a way out. That is the tradition of theatre. The authors of antiquity dealt with the myths in their competitions, striving to tell the stories in such different ways that they could earn the prize. The competition was not artistic-aesthetic, but how do I tell my story so that the polis has today, in the moment of performance, something different to discuss than last time, and that is more interesting than the story my competitor tells. This making-public of contradictions that are meant to be hidden away. If we stay with *Mother Courage* for a moment, of course there are, after such a horrible war, quite natural, human, not a priori objectionable tendency that we want to leave all that behind us now—I just cannot think of it any more. But in little bits you have to think of these things again and again, because without that you cannot progress. This is a technique of thinking. With his dialectics of contradiction, Brecht gave this energy to resist this uniform reality that was infused with ideology, was eliminated, was spirited away. He used to tell his stories always in such way that the people thought them through to the end.

My directing work echoes Brecht's episodic structure where every scene carries a social message presented as a social dialectic. But as Brecht would say: reality alters; to represent it the means of representation must alter, too.

With Brecht, the actors had to develop a different kind of readiness to find ways of being a collaborator and to listen. This made rehearsals sometimes extremely long. As a result, some actors withdrew from Brecht or were afraid that it might get too theoretical for them. The difficulty is that some actors are not well educated, and that the school system under the emperor, in the Weimar Republic and under the Nazis never taught dialectic thinking as an enjoyable activity, as entertainment, although in the 1920s much of culture was created in that direction.

What is beautiful about both Stanislavski and Brecht is how taken for granted the principle of the ensemble. The influence of any one methodology would have been much more evident in the achievements of the ensemble, in the productions, as a result. I remembers having seen some very old Tairov productions, real museum pieces that toured, and it was evident how the artistes—I am not saying actors—were able to fulfil to 100% what the system demanded. I also saw some dreadful productions of the Moscow Art Theatre, which had to do with the plays themselves, propaganda plays which he was forced to do, but in these, too, you could see how different the approach was. If you are used to consider things as strange, different, unusual, as something that is potentially in contrast or in conflict with yourself, then you are able to detect beauty. It is one of those beauties that organisations of this kind are able to develop a system. Suzuki demonstrates that it takes years to train in the system. Thus I do not speak out against Stanislavski. I do, however, try to define the actor as something other than the vehicle of my private feelings and intentions, and I did not need him to survive in the GDR—I need Brecht to survive. There may be situations where Stanislavski is exactly right.

If I am interested in how anything that develops does so in a social context I open up different perspectives, but those do not object to other people's perspectives. In the family of actors there are different degrees to which attention, being considerate to and having respect for each other can work even if people come together from different directions if they have the appropriate level of humility towards their common object, which is the theatre. The theatre is the orchestra, is the special chance for survival that you are offered if you are allowed to go on to the stage. That is what I try to teach my acting students, to become attentive, alert contemporaries who note and notice each other. They need an awareness of things besides the strictly defined craft that Stanislavski was so concerned about.

DMD
Could you comment on a director's style?

HUH
I find style boring. It is always developed in relation to oneself. I want to demonstrate my demarcations against someone else. I want to be this way and not that way. I can teach and learn that quite quickly and it is empty, especially when I repeat it. What for? In the arts, new styles have always been defined after the event. Those who are credited with "inventing" a new style did not only practice that style alone. In my own case I have adopted a certain way of thinking from Brecht and try to use it responsibly. The key to that way if thinking is what I have been referring to again and again in this interview: to note and collect contradictions and to gain joy and pleasure in that, and to represent oddities and perversions of human existence. It may be the case that certain aesthetic patterns are repeated, but that is not the same as style. Every one of Brecht's productions was different—not, however, because he had decided to do it differently, but in response to political events. In GDR times, masks on stage were actually not permitted, so as to avoid any danger of formalism. This remained a kind of agreement of aesthetics between Goebbels and Ulbricht. In that situation, after *Mother Courage* with its grey-green costumes, Brecht did *Caucasian Chalk Circle*, with masks, decorated with pearls, costumes cut in line with Indian garments, light, from silk, with shades of watercolours, the stage richly decorated as in 1001 nights. He organised a programme brochure in which the leader of the theatre's workshop complained that he was unable to get any more buttons and clasps—all manufacturers of buttons and clasps had been closed down or had been integrated into the VEB system. Helene Weigel published an exchange of letters: Brecht had just chosen a motif from Picasso for the curtain. The *Neues Deutschland* ran an agitation and propaganda piece in which West Berlin workers uttered their anger: we come to the democratic sector of Berlin and what do we have to see: a formalist image in the BE. What are those splodges for—they are not proper faces as we, the working classes, want to see them. Helene Weigel published a letter she had received from Berlin: Dear Helene, we sold your 150 posters with the Picasso masks and sent the money we made to the resistance fighters in Indonesia.

The culture of Brecht is of course different from that of the municipal theatre. Brecht's overarching term and concept was "thinking capable of intervention". This concept implies an openness that allows you to work with any aesthetic material. Brecht was clever enough to demonstrate action capable of intervention in relation to thought capable of intervention. This has nothing to do with Brecht the poet, the author, the man of the theatre who made his compromise with the devil, who was run-down—all the things he was accused of. He was all of those, to be sure, and I always knew that—but that's not the point. If during times of dictatorship you select your therapy against that background, you won't find anything. You won't find anything in real life unless you have got the stamina to see what I can use as long as I can still justify it to myself. This is a considerable contradiction in Brecht: someone who thinks more dialectically than he behaves. On the other hand it is very easy to sit in judgment and to be the one to throw the first stone. It never occurred to me, in those early years, although I knew it very well. It did not have to occur to me because I was never a communist, because from the start, naturally and organically I was anti-communist.

When I told people they were surprised that there were any anti-communists in the GDR—for them it was only Löwenthal[23] who was anti-communist. Of course that's also the wrong answer: thank God there was at least *one* anti-communist in the ZDF, Löwenthal; he was an honourable man, who today is acknowledged by his own party and his own circles only somewhat coyly. The only reason why he was not totally vilified in the West was because he was a Jew. I was acutely aware of this falsehood, and I suffered from it, but people consider it unimportant and they do not wish to know anything about it. If you do not want to know about all these things, you just cannot go on the stage, because you cannot reduce yourself to the level of prostitution—which a lot of this profession amounts to.

What I tell my students is they now you are at that stage in your lives when you buy the last books. After that nothing will have that much meaning again. You can make a lot with only three or four books. You have to read them, you have to play with the material, bring into play all the things you experience in books. Then it is wealth. Once real life sets in, all this is only an apercus. The intensity you can experience as a young person is what you need to make use of.

DMD

How would you describe the director's responsibility towards the actor? Is there a limit up to which the director may make demand on and challenge the actor?

HUH

The director must make demands on the actors in relation to everything that is playful, must engage them with what is playful. Every kind of sultry proximity is unprofessional. Any intimacy must be avoided. It is a different matter that intimacy can always develop in the context of the theatre. However, the director as the one who leads the work process carries the responsibility and can avail himself of that responsibility by continuously making new suggestions for play, thus engaging the actors in a mode of thinking that allows the actors to forget themselves in that respect. As an actor I too often experienced how through inappropriate psychology, how closeness, originating from laziness, was supposed to solve problems. Theatre is indeed a fertile soil for such wrong developments, because the nerves and the feelings and the soul are bared, You have to be aware of it and have to objectify it, but that is not an intellectual process. It only works if you get each other into the enjoyable mode of discovery, to discover what is worth discovering, what is so unusual, scurrilous, so that the actor then risks things and to share secrets with the director in telling an even minute aspect of the story. This does not involve an overlap of private and artistic levels. I admit that this is a difficult process—here and there, overlaps may be possible. However, these unintentional overlaps are never the means to trigger some special feelings or daredevil action. Trust and closeness are only possible through distance. You have to organise a situation, or rather the conditions, in which the other person admits to you that he hasn't got anything in his trouser pockets. As the director you have to take the lead. You have to organise that an attention develops within the actors, allowing them to notice it. You cannot organise anything irrespective of the existing conditions. As a result you have to painstakingly refer the actors back to the play, to the telling of the story, thus arriving at suggestions for play. You don't achieve this by talking and preaching and forming little sects. In general I tend to find off-off-off theatre unbearable because it is sectarian—all those with a green political perspective go to this theatre only. They play only for greens. No: theatre is for banker and porter, grandmother and child, fat and slim, thick and clever. This mix is what you need to keep in mind, it provides the quarry for the emotional memory. As director I have to stimulate the actors to gather from there to enable and enrich their acting. Again: never l'art pour l'art, but always in the service of telling stories.

Here is a quote from the Schiller-Goethe correspondence: "A dramatic plot will move before my eyes. An epic seems to stand still while I move around it. I can linger or hurry according to my own subjective needs. I can take a step backwards or leap ahead, and so forth." This is Schiller's concept of the epic. Brecht did not approach it in this way, because it did not serve his purposes.

DMD

In Germany and in the UK there is a tendency, within the context of political correctness, to show, in the theatre, violence, excess, gratuitous nudity. I ask myself how these relate to the actor's human dignity.

HUH

I fully agree. I do not understand how actors can go ahead with all this. I am stunned when I see the extent to which directing in the theatre has deteriorated to these excesses. These directors are either ideologists or they are absolutely socially irresponsible. This is what I wrote on this topic recently in my introduction to a book about Yeats:

"A left salvation army made up of ego-addicted despots of directing, of dramaturges who hate the audience and of pubescent authors seizes the boards that once represented the world and terrorises the audience with its excesses of emptiness and disgust with life. For them the future has been inhabited already to the point of advanced wear and tear, they do not have any field of projection any more for collective desires because they reject the intrinsic purpose of the art. They invoke their panic grief or their political pain and put themselves up as professional agitators".

DMD

And then a critic like Stadelmayer[24] writes against this and he is attacked across Germany.

HUH

It was under pains and great efforts and against trouble with the Stasi that as a young man I got *Theater Heute* from the West. Today I hardly read it because if I do it bores me. Over the years a tone has developed that I would characterise as nonchalant sullenness, as elitist lateral thinking which does not aim at anything, or describe anything that would serve to represent, in terms of theatre practice, hope, the family nature of theatre, the overarching processes involved in theatre, as constructive and friendly.

What the critics are creating are the most private spaces of utterance. They are disillusioned with West Germany, no matter who is chancellor, Schröder or Merkel; their horizon is very restricted. For me it is irresponsible. This is reflected, to a large extent, by academic research and writing. I tend to react aggressively because there is no basis in a friendly attitude to life. They lack the ability to develop overarching connections. Most of current writing does not even touch on the ways people or theatre function—rather they deal with themselves. Fine, if that's what the market needs today—an I participate in that market, for fun, so that I might be able to show my Dean, who comes from Maths, that I, too, can write. For most current academic writing it takes me a lot of trouble to get through the bulk of hubris to reach to the small point someone may have to contribute.

The scenes you mentioned earlier do not have any impact in the true sense, but they develop bondage, which is the precise opposite of what directing in the theatre should really achieve. Theatre in the Greek sense was meant to make the members of society independent, self-determined. The actor's task is to lead others to self-determination. This is what the classics are all about.

Notes

1 Heinz-Uwe Haus (b. 1942) trained as an actor at the Filmhochschule Potsdam Babelsberg and began his professional career as an actor at the theatres in Senftenberg, then Brandenburg. He moved to Berlin to work as master disciple with Manfred Wekwerth at the Deutsches Theater, where he was the youngest director even on the theatre's directing staff. Wekwerth later invited Haus to join him at the Institut für Schauspielregie in Berlin, where he became Wekwerth's deputy and leader of the directing section. An opponent against the communist regime from his earliest years, Haus had frequent trouble with the authorities. He was allowed to direct abroad, mainly in Greece and Cyprus, also in the USA. In the late 1980s, Haus became politically active in the movement that led to the end of the GDR. Haus continues to direct and give lectures and workshops world-wide. Since 1997, Haus has held a professorship at the University of Delaware, USA. A "Festschrift" for Heinz-Uwe Haus, edited by Daniel Meyer-Dinkgräfe, is scheduled for publication with Cambridge Scholars Press for 2007 on the occasion of Haus's 65th birthday.
2 Arthur Pohl (1900-1970), German film director.
3 Ilse Steppat (1917-1969), German stage and film actress; she played Irma Bunt in the James Bond movie *On Her Majesty's Secret Service*.
4 Steffie Spira (1908-1995), German stage and film actress.
5 Arno Paulsen (1900-1969), German stage and film actor who also worked in dubbing (the German voice of Oliver Hardy, among others).

6 Karl Hellmer (1896-1974), German stage and film actor.

7 DEFA (Deutsche Film Aktiengesellschaft) was the state-monopolised film production company in the German Democratic Republic.

8 The closest in the English context is police chief inspector or detective superintendent.

9 Wolfgang Heinz (1900-1984), Austrian actor, director and Intendant.

10 Walter Ulbricht (1893-1973), was first secretary of the Socialist Unity Party of the GDR from 1950-1971.

11 Benno Besson (1922-2006), Swiss theatre actor and director. Brecht invited him to join him in Berlin at the Berliner Ensemble in 1949.

12 Manfred Wekwerth (b. 1929), German director. He trained as a teacher and was discovered by Brecht in an amateur theatre company. After Brecht's death, Wekwerth was chief director at the Berliner Ensemble from 1960 to 1969; in 1974 he founded the Institut für Schauspielregie in Berlin. In 1977 he became Intendant at the BE. In 1982 he was elected president of the Berlin Akademie der Künste. From 1986-89 he was member of the SED's central committee.

13 Hans-Anselm Perten (1917-1984), Intendant of the Deutsches Theater from 1970-72, formerly Intendant of the Volkstheater Rostock.

14 Gerhard Wolfram (1922-1991) was Intendant of the Deutsches Theater 1972-82.

15 Martin Niemöller (1892-1984) was a prominent German protestant theologist.

16 Johnnie Carson (1925-2005), American entertainer, hosted "The Tonight Show" from 1962-1992.

17 Harald Juhnke (1929-2005), German actor, singer and entertainer.

18 Alexander Moissi (1879-1925). Born in Albania, Moissi settled in Vienna at the age of twenty, where he was supported by the actor Josef Kainz (1958-1910). Moissi later worked much with Max Reinhardt. (1873-1943).

19 Major von Tellheim is the main male character in *Minna von Barnhelm*, a comedy by Gotthold Ephraim Lessing (1729-1781).

20 *The Government Inspector* by Nikolai Gogol (1809-1852).

21 Georg von Saxe Meiningen (1826-1914) revolutionised theatre practice with his emphasis on historical realism of sets and costumes, and with increased emphasis on acting.

22 Erich Honecker (1912-1994), led the GDR from 1971-1989.

23 Gerhard Löwenthal (1922-2002), German holocaust survivor and conservative journalist, who presented the "ZDF Magazin" from 1969-1988.

24 Gerhard Stadelmaier (b.1950), is the chief theatre critic for the Frankfurter Allgemeine Zeitung.

CHAPTER TWENTY-FOUR

PERSONAL LEGACY:
URSULA DINKGRÄFE

Ursula Dinkgräfe (b. 1927) in interview with DMD, August 2006

DMD
What is your first memory of theatre?

UD
My first memory of theatre is from Hannover. It was in winter [1932], so I must have been five years old. I saw a fairy tale, called *The Doll Fairy*, and I remember how a dancer dressed as a doll emerged from a large cardboard box and danced on pointe on top of the box. That was wonderful, yes, that was beauty; that was my first impression of beauty. In Klein-Lessen [from 1933 onwards] I started writing my own plays, very short, a page or two each, collected in a school exercise book, and to rehearse them with Lore [Eleonore Hoffmann née Plate, her cousin]. Sometimes we had performances in front of the adults. On one occasion we rehearsed a play about knights, for which we had prepared shields from wood, and my father had painted coats of arms onto them. But during the dress rehearsal we smashed the shields, so we could not proceed to the performance proper.

Probably also inspired by the ballet I had seen in Hannover, I did some training in acrobatics with Lore. We managed, after a lot of effort, to get some ballet shoes, which Ilse [one of her aunts] sent from Paris. Black ones for me and pink ones for Lore. Those were the only ones available in our sizes. Hella [Lore's mother] had sewn pink ballet tutus for us from silk, and we did a dance performance.

At school we also rehearsed plays and put them on. I remember on one occasion I played a small child. I had the first lines of the play: "And I don't want to and I don't like to, I am not at all keen; let me go, mother, open the door, I want to get away". On the day of the performance, however, I was ill, but I was collected by car from home and taken to the pub where the performance took place. I played my scene and then I was wrapped up again and taken home.

As part of my compulsory service in the BDM[1], I attended a camp holiday, at the end of which we presented a play. In later years, towards the end of the 2nd World War, when the hospitals were full of wounded soldiers, I was BDM leader and instead of doing the usual kind of stuff they required us to do, I rehearsed plays with the girls in my charge and we went to the hospitals and field hospitals and performed there.

DMD
What kinds of plays did you show?

UD
Fairy tales, such as *Cinderalla*. The soldiers liked that. Where they were up to it, we performed entire plays. But on one occasion the sister came up to us and told us that the soldiers on her ward were very ill and could not endure an entire performance. So we shortened our play. I narrated the plot, and each one of the actors only said a few lines here and there. Just before the end of the war I went for one last performance to a field hospital all on my own and on the way back there was an air raid alarm in the area prior to the allied troupes coming in, but I managed to get home safely. At the end of that visit I was asked to return to one of the soldiers I had performed to; he was a journalist, a very well-known one, who said thank you to me again, adding that I had restored his belief in life with my performance.

DMD
How old were you in those days, and how old were the other girls?

UD
I started my work in this when I was around fourteen, fifteen. The other girls were both my own age, but some of them were also older, around eighteen.

DMD
How did your decision to work as an actor professionally develop?

UD
Also just at the end of the war, there was a musical competition in Celle, and I recited a poem in local dialect and presented the opening soliloquy

of Goethe's *Iphigenia*. The competition was run by Heinrich Koch[2], an important theatre maker, who was head of the drama school in Celle. I was very successful there, Koch said to me I must become an actress and join him in Celle.

DMD

Wasn't it your mother who had coached you in recitation?

UD

Yes, my mother taught recitation to both myself and to Lore. Poems, in the local dialect, expression and intonation.

The local newspaper carried a long article about my performance at the musical competition. After the war, Heinrich Koch probably didn't want to know anything more from me, perhaps because he did not wish to be associated with that musical competition, which was still held under the Nazis.

Also towards the end of the war I had travelled to Meiningen, to visit an aunt, and one of the friends of that aunt's family was an actor for whom I auditioned, and he thought I was gifted and should become an actress. I then mentioned my desire to become an actress to another aunt, in Bremen; she told me that the actor Herbert Sebald[3] was living not too far away from her and he had acting students, he was a private acting teacher. She knew because one of her tenants took lessons from him. I went home and told my parents that I wanted to take lessons. They withdrew for their daily nap after lunch and when they emerged from it they told me that they approved. I auditioned for Sebald and he accepted me. He said that I had to work a lot, but he saw the potential and the talent.

DMD

What was that training like?

UD

At first *Der Kleine Hai*, a collection of voice and pronunciation exercises, then studying roles. The first was Hedvig from Ibsen's *The Wild Duck*. I had to learn the part by heart, he gave me the cues, and I played for him, and he worked it through with me. I went there once a week, for one hour. After a year of lessons, Sebald told me that he felt I didn't make any more progress and I should see more live theatre. Then I auditioned at the *Niederdeutsche Bühne* in Bremen and immediately got a full-time contract. I looked for a room to live in, and found a small room, with some bomb damage, there was a gap to the open air under the bed, perhaps an inch wide. There was no coal available that year, and I went off to steal coal from trains in the railway station, every now and then, just like many other people. I had to do so much work at the theatre that I had hardly time left to continue my lessons. Sebald saw me and told me that now I was showing all the things he had felt had been missing when I acted for him during his lessons. Then I auditioned for Gillis van Rappard[4] at the *Künstlertheater* in Bremen. He found me promising but advised me to abandon acting in dialect. So I resigned from the *Niederdeutsches Theater*, and got freelance work, first of all with the *Kammerspiele* in Bremen where I played Becky in *Our Town*. Elfriede Kuzmany[5] was a brilliant Emily. Rappard saw that production and approved of my work and so I got freelance employment at his *Künstlertheater* as well.

DMD

In those years, how many weeks of rehearsals were the norm per production, and hours per day?

UD

There were no rules in those days, especially with Rappard, endless rehearsals, dress rehearsal all day long. There were usually four weeks per production, sometimes, with Rappard, five. I also worked with a group of actors with whom I toured the area. When we arrived at our performance venues, I would usually set up our mobile lighting, while the men went for a meal. Another theatre in Bremen were I worked was the *Theater im Hause*, a small venue attached to a villa. I remember one production that took place over summer—the windows were open and we could hear the birds singing in the park outside, and this made for a wonderful atmosphere. In *Der Erste Frühlingstag* I remember I had a very poetic scene, I had to sit on a wall, was a bit dreamy, a bit in love. I was wearing a dress I had to provide myself for the production, but they sewed it for me, made from parachute silk which we had taken from crashed planes.

DMD

You took your official final test as an actress twice.

UD

Yes, I took the first one in 1947, with Rappard as the examiner, and he told me then that I should stop performing in local dialect and take the exams again in a year's time. A year later I had performed a lot in the other theatres in Bremen and I went to Hannover to take the final exams again. I had written a long letter to go with it, auditioned, and it all went very quickly and I passed.

DMD

Over your career you had quite a number of contracts with different theatres. What were the kinds of reasons that led you to leave one place and move on to another one?

UD

The reasons varied. When I was in Bremen, performing as a guest artist with different local theatres, Wolf Rathjen[6], the artistic director of the chamber theatre in Solingen had seen me in the *Theater in Hause* in Bremen, and he approached me and offered me a one-year contract in Solingen. Later, Rappard, who had worked with me in Bremen, had moved on to Detmold and arranged for me to come there as a visiting artist for one production, as Portia in *The Merchant of Venice*. While I was in Solingen, I auditioned at the Westdeutscher Rundfunk, the radio company in Cologne. I got some work there, and on one occasion I worked with Elisabeth Flickenschild[7], who was in Gründgens[8,] company in Düsseldorf. One day she just said to me: "On Tuesday next week you will audition for Gründgens, I have arranged it." She gave me the details, and added "Make sure you are on time". When I arrived, I was led into Gründgens's office, and I was welcomed by Gorski[9], his personal assistant. He looked a little like Gründgens, with bald head and glasses, so I mistook him for Gründgens at first and was very deferential to him. Gorski told me that there were another two young actresses auditioning that day, and I would have to wait. One of the other two was a little smaller than me, also with red hair; she was the daughter of a well-known actress. The other one was the grand-daughter of German author Hermann Hesse. Then the actor Jürgen Goslar[10] came out of Gründgens's office and told me that Gründgens had mentioned that there were three young actresses to audition and he could not make up his mind whom to take. So Goslar advised him to take all three. The first to audition on stage was the one with the famous mother, and she disappeared. She must have been too weak. Then Hesse's grand-daughter, she was asked to wait, so she was not sent away as the first one had been. Then it was my turn; I had prepared Hedvig from *The Wild Duck*; Gründgens was happy with just that one speech and said "Thank you, thank you, that's enough". So I thought that I was not successful. But I was not sent away, but was asked to stay on and wait. Hans Müller Westernhagen[11] was around, and I told him about my problems of not being able to get back to Solingen that evening because the last train had already gone. He and his wife offered me to sleep on the sofa in their living room once I was done. While I had to wait, Gründgens spent a long time with Hesse's granddaughter, talked to her, worked with her on the stage, and finally offered her employment. Very late that evening he asked me into his office and said: "I want to employ you. How much do you earn now?" I told him DM 125; so he said: "So let's say DM 350". It was a small salary, but still. That was all, and I could go to the Müller Westernhagens to sleep on their sofa in the living room. They had a dog and it was sick in the night, in the living room, it was awful.

In the summer break after the first season with Gründgens, I took some riding lessons, at the suggestion of Maximilian Schell[12]. I had a fall, and broke my symphysis, the bone that combines both parts of the pelvis. In Düsseldorf they thought that it would take a long time for me to get better, and also that I would probably not be able to walk properly any more. Usually when the symphysis is injured, people are left with a limp, because one leg ends up shorter. In my case there was a 1cm difference, when the bones had grown together again. But after six weeks of lying still, as soon as I was allowed to move again I did yoga exercises; some time later they took another x-ray and there was no longer any difference left. Düsseldorf had planned to cast me in a wonderful, major part in *Das Kleine Teehaus*, but I had not recovered in time, and so they did not schedule me for anything at all for a long time. I was free and sought, and got, work in Frankfurt at the Kleines Theater im Zoo, led by Fritz Rémond[13]. It was in Frankfurt that an agent, Mrs. Meyer, saw me and liked a lot what she saw, and must have told Gründgens, also that I was walking perfectly normally. Then they went back to giving me parts.

After three seasons I resigned from Gründgens because I wanted to play more classical parts. I got a full-time contract with the theatre in Heidelberg, starting off with a part in the summer festival, which took place at the castle. After that production followed the summer break, which I spent in the company of a yoga teacher, travelling through Germany in a tiny Messerschmitt car; we passed through Bayreuth, were he knew some people at the Festival, so we were able to watch a number of performances from somewhere backstage. The productions we saw included *Tannhäuser* with Gré Brouwenstijn[14], and one production with Wolfgang Windgassen[15]. In Heidelberg, after the summer break, I started off as Miranda in *The Tempest*. Then I went to Frankfurt to Rémond, who cast me as Agnes in Molière's *School for Wives*, and while I played in Frankfurt in the evenings I rehearsed Abigail in Scribe's *The Glass of Water* in Heidelberg during the days.

Then I played for a few productions in Hannover. After Hannover I got a guest contract at the Komödie in Stuttgart, with Berthold Sakmann[16]. For my part there I needed my hair a stronger red than they had naturally. So I went to the hairdressers and came back with a hair colour that was bright red veering to pink, so strong that people turned when they saw me in the street. Sakmann would have liked to keep me on for more work but I already held a contract for the Luisenburg-festival in Wundsiedel, where I played Ophelia. In a long and arduous procedure the bright red had to be taken out of my hair—I ended up medium blond, and with that hair colour I played Ophelia.

In 1959 I played Gretchen in Ingolstadt. When I auditioned for the part, there was another actress auditioning as well. I was still very fat, from my recent pregnancy. The other actress was very slim. The artistic director told me later that she looked very sweet, but her audition was not very good at all. The actor who played Faust was tall and bulky, so we were suited to each other.

The artistic director in Heidelberg had already wanted to keep me in Heidelberg. He had in the meantime moved to Kiel, where he now invited me to join him. When I arrived there, with my medium-blond hair and still too fat from the pregnancy, I remember how the director's wife saw me and was shocked. I was just not at all how they had thought I would look: I looked younger, and with unsuitably dyed hair. I was scheduled to play a large part, as a more mature woman, but they changed their casting quickly and I played the small part of a young girl, very suitably so. After one year in Kiel I was invited to join the theatre in Wilhelmshaven, where I stayed for two seasons. I had to leave because my mother could not take care of you any more on her own.

A year later I sought employment, through audition, in Cuxhaven. Towards the end of the season in Cuxhaven the artistic director was not able to pay me more money, which I simply needed to survive, I had gone without sufficient food for some weeks during my year there already, especially while playing Iphigenia, and had suffered some heart problems as a result. So I sought work elsewhere, and was employed in Flensburg. I left there after one very unhappy year, both as far as our living conditions were concerned, and the working conditions. We moved to Oldenburg. The artistic director, Wilhelm List-Diehl[17], was looking for an actress to take over some of the parts otherwise reserved for his wife. There, at the end of four seasons, List-Diehl, moved on to Konstanz but did not want to take me with him, and the new artistic director in Oldenburg, Harry Niemann[18], brought most of his company with him from where he had been before. So I was unemployed for a year until I auditioned for the job in Neuss. I stayed there for five seasons, before the artistic director in Neuss, Hermann Wetzke[19], decided not to renew my contract. The reason was never fully explained. An actress of my own age, a rival, if you like, had done some stints as a guest artist in Neuss. She was well connected in the area, and once I had been fired, she was employed full-time. Wetzke may also have been hurt because we called your pet Hamster Hermann... From then on I worked freelance at theatres in the area that did not operate full-time, all-year employment but hired actors by production, which would not run in repertory, but ensuite.

DMD
You mentioned unfortunate living conditions in Flensburg. Across your career, you must have seen quite a range of accommodation...

UD
In Solingen, Rathjen and I lived on the top floor of an old large house; the owner was a middle-aged, very untidy and incredibly fat woman. She suddenly had a baby; she didn't know she was pregnant, so it was a surprise. We had two rooms on the top floor, first I had the room on the left, the smaller one, but it did not have any heating. He had a larger room, on the right. Then it turned winter, and cold, and no heating. So I got a larger room on a lower floor, it had a stove that I could use, with coal, to heat the room. The large room had a huge window facing the stadium; it was on the first floor, so no-one could look in. It didn't have any curtains. The bed was under the window, so I could gaze at the stars.

In Wilhelmshaven at first I lived in a guesthouse, but it was noisy, facing a trunk road. I moved to a little room, which was not very nice either, and my rental contract was terminated early because I used to get back home late after performances. I then found a very nice room in a house a little further away from the theatre. The house was good and new, my room was right at the top and separate from the rest of the house.

The theatre in Hannover toured its productions in the area, and I remember that in the evenings I had to walk back from the theatre to the place where I lived through a wooded area. It was always a little bit of an adventure, but also poetic, and not dangerous in those days. In Wunsiedel, when I played Ophelia, I was some months pregnant already but it didn't show too much. The landlady of the place where I lived noticed that I was pregnant, probably because of my morning sickness. I had a little one-burner stove in my rented room, where I could cook my soup, and on one occasion she baked a meal of pastry for me, to cheer me up.

In Cuxhaven we first lived with friends of a housekeeper of one of my aunts, and then we moved to rented accommodation, first an upstairs bedroom, then a basement flat. They had shortage of accommodation in Flensburg; the only place that was available for us to live was a ground floor flat in a housing estate. The neighbours to the right were nice. To the left the neighbours had many children, some of them very unpredictably aggressive. The neighbours in the flat above were a lorry driver and his wife, their son, and a grandmother who used to empty her pisspot out of her window into our garden. In Oldenburg we lived on the 3rd, top floor of a block of flats. In the flat below, for the first year or so, lived one of the violinists of the theatre, with his wife, a singer, he later gave you violin classes and I took singing lessons with her. We only got a flat in the first place when my mother agreed to sign the contract—they were suspicious of a single mother with son, and an artist as well. The place was filthy, and I had to spend many hours scrubbing it clean. When we moved out four years later, the flat was spotless, of course, but the owner of the block of flats came in person to inspect whether we would leave the flat in an acceptable state. During my freelance years from 1975-87 I had to spend much time travelling, staying in hotels or temporary accommodation. I remember on one occasion I had to share a flat with one of the other two colleagues in a three-hander. My room had only a thick curtain to the hall, no proper door, and I was able to hear my colleague when her boyfriend came to visit. Quite embarrassing and not so nice, really. In one hotel room, in the mid-1980s, during the winter, the water in the sink was frozen…

DMD
Over those last years, you had to travel a lot, with some adventures:

UD
While employed at the Kleines Theater Bad Godesberg, a female colleague and I once missed a train home; we had to spend some five hours in the middle of the night on the railway station in Cologne, in the waiting room. Railway police came through every now and then and asked us whether we were fine. There were some quite unsavoury characters around, but about an hour before our train was due, I saw a group of younger men coming in, who grouped together not too far away from us, and then I saw that another man somewhere else in the waiting room winked at the group and nodded in our direction. I immediately said to my colleague that we had to leave and go to the station this instant. Fortunately I must have been so intense when I said this that she

immediately followed, without asking. I never felt afraid in tense situations—I tended to be angry, but at that time I was really afraid. A couple of times public transport let me down, and I reached the performance venue minutes before my scheduled entrance on stage. That was quite nerve-racking, mainly for myself, but also for colleagues already on stage.

DMD
Tell me more about what is was like combining single motherhood with your career.

UD
In 1958, in Hannover I met Michael Chevalier, your father, and after Ophelia I could not perform any more until after you were born. So I moved to Munich. Sakmann insisted on seeing me there, and offered me a part for a tour to South America. He suggested taking the baby there with me. But I decided it was too dangerous after all.

While I played Gretchen in Ingolstadt I was still living in Munich, my mother took care of you, and I commuted to the rehearsals and performances from Munich to Ingolstadt on a daily basis. You were with me the year I spent in Kiel, and in the evenings for performances, or during rehearsals, I left you at home, asking a neighbour in the flat below to have a look if she heard you crying. That happened only once in that entire year, though.

In Wilhelmshaven I first played in *Der Eingebildete Kranke* as guest artist. They liked my work very much and I got the offer of a full-time contract. My mother took care of you, and I paid for her to take on a helper in the house. I could have stayed in Wilhelmshaven for a third season. I had very good reviews from a Mr Hildebrandt, and had met his wife, and we had become friends. She offered me to take you in to life with the family, for me to come over at any time as much as I wanted in my spare time. My mother did not agree to this, very strongly, and so I stayed with her, my sister and yourself for one season, before I got the contract with Cuxhaven, where I took you with me right from the start.

In Cuxhaven I first registered you with the Protestant kindergarten, but they didn't take much care of the children, who were all running around without supervision. There was one larger boy there with behavioural problems, quite aggressive, sometimes, and there was a very dangerous entrance, on that kindergarten's premises, to a cellar. So I took you out of there immediately and registered you in the Catholic kindergarten instead. It was run by nuns, and you seemed quite happy there. On one occasion they wanted to give you pickled herring salad with mayonnaise to eat. You told them you did not want to eat it and that you would have to throw up if you did. They insisted, and you did throw up. We had very nice neighbours there, and you stayed with them a lot and played with their son, who was your age. On one occasion you had come down with the flu, and the landlady offered for a friend of her's to take care of you. But you didn't like her at all, and spat into her face. She never came again. In Flensburg the nice neighbours to one side of our flat had a daughter who worked as a hairdresser, and she looked after you sometimes. In Oldenburg we had nice neighbours across the road, where you went for lunch after school when I was at rehearsals.

DMD
How would you describe the many directors you worked with?

UD
The director in Detmold, where I played Portia in *The Merchant of Venice*, was not good: he did not support me as I would have needed it. I asked Rappard to help me, but he refused: he didn't want to interfere with his colleague's work. The other women in the cast were not very friendly, so it was a tough time for me. There was one good review, but also some not so good ones, and they were right, I must say. I was not nuanced enough; there was feeling there, from my inside, but the form I was able to give to that feeling was not so good. I didn't feel well or secure.

In Düsseldorf, my first role was Leontine in *Der Biberpelz*. Ulrich Erfurth[20] directed. He told me at the first rehearsal that I didn't have to play the social accusation of all humankind. Gründgens had not seen any rehearsals and come on stage just before the opening night and said to me "Make sure you don't bring shame on me". Nice, isn't it? But I was good, and had good reviews. In Düsseldorf I played one of the girls in *Herrenhaus*. I had to dance, and the others who played the girls were slow and didn't know what to do, so Gründgens told them to look at me and do what I did. Later I played a countess, and without any text I had to walk across the stage, from left to right, all on my own, without anything else happening on stage. Then I played Pnina in *Der Drachenthron*; Gründgens cast that play against type. He told me to imagine I was Yvonne de Carlo[21]. After that rehearsal I went home and padded myself out and moved around at home as Yvonne de Carlo, and rehearsed my lines in that style. The next day he was very impressed. I was given a black wig and was padded out. There was an older colleague in the company, who did not recognise me at the opening night. Gründgens instructed me to play the characteristics of the part very strongly at first, so that the audience knew what I was aiming at, and to reduce my intensity later. Some of the younger members of the company were allowed to sit in on Gründgens's rehearsals for *Wallenstein*. On one occasion he turned round to us and, pointing to the stage, asked us what was wrong on the stage. He was getting up and on his way to go to the stage. On stage a number of the actors were standing in a row, and one actor was slightly out of line. I had noticed that and told Gründgens when he asked us. He agreed that this was what had been bothering him, too. Gründgens always was very witty in his comments and explanations while directing, how he suggested this or that be played. It was a joy just listening to that. In principle he knew what he wanted. He did not experiment, but he changed, worked through the scenes.

With Rémond in Frankfurt, you had to come with text fully learnt by heart. He did not first block and then rehearse, he went straight into rehearsal. It always worked out fine. As a matter of principle he never used a prompt, neither for rehearsals nor for performances. He himself did not know his lines that well, actually. He knew the frame, but often he launched himself into long speeches, which were not in the text of the play, but which made sense in the context. His partners had to be very flexible to respond appropriately, and to try to find back to the scripted text. I was able to do that quite well, and he liked that about me. Later, from Heidelberg, I went back to Rémond to play Luise in Schiller's *Kabale und Liebe* on tour in South America. He rehearsed all parts individually with the actors, with blocking and expression, because we were not able to come together due to other commitments. On the plane to South America we had the first chance of reading through our scenes with the other actors. We arrived at Buenos Aires, where we had to set up our stage ourselves. The stage was so huge that we closed the curtain and put up our set in front of it, where the space was still too large. During the performances I was also in charge of the props, and for the first performance I remember I had to keep rushing from the dressing rooms, which were miles away from the stage, where the props were kept in boxes, to the stage and back. Altogether the first performance took an hour longer than the following ones because everything was so new; the actress who played Lady Milford, required most of the time we had available for rehearsals on the first day, so most scenes were first performed on the opening night.

Before casting me as Adela in *Bernarda Alba's House* the artistic director in Kiel asked me whether I thought I could cope with that part. I said "yes, of course", and I was indeed very successful. In Wilhelmshaven the artistic director was Rudolf Stromberg; he was exceptionally competent and confident, totally unbiased and professional. He directed many productions himself. The other major director at the theatre was gay, which, for women in particular, is often very good in the context of the theatre. He was small, very alert, a very good, patient and kind director. We had a costume designer there, who worked literally day and night to make genuinely wonderful costumes. They were totally suitable to the plays for which they were made. Working in Wilhelmshaven was great, all people were nice, and there was a good feeling in the company.

In Cuxhaven, *Iphigenia* was a very good production, directed by the artistic director, Toni Graschberger. At the beginning of the rehearsal process he told us that were not going to play the definitive *Iphigenia*, but "just" one production of the play, but we were all very good. He worked with me very well, very thoroughly, he supported me with the text, helped me to imagine Iphigenia's situation, her feelings, while he provided a lot of historical background. Polly in *Threepenny Opera* was particularly wonderful in Cuxhaven because the stage had a low ceiling and we set the play in a theatre's costume collection. They put hooks in the ceiling and costumes were hanging down all over the place, leaving, of course, sufficient space for us to play. But it created a very special atmosphere. The colleague who played Macheath was very special, too, a little like a tramp, a little brutal and a little soft. Dagmar Soerensen was Jenny, and her singing was great. I, too, had to sing songs, and had coaching for that. My voice was sufficient and even good for the small space.

The first production in Flensburg was the Lady in *Kabale und Liebe*. I had Inge Langen's[22] way of playing that part in my mind, from the Frankfurt – Rémond tour to South America. So I was really very good and secure at the first rehearsal, but the director was awful. He asked me to cut of this sentence, to add a pause here, to give that word a different emphasis, or this sentence a different intonation. He managed to pick apart my entire intuition into intellectual thinking. As a result I was unable to play any longer; constantly I had to keep thinking: what am I supposed to emphasise here, or there. In addition I had a very poor costume in the first scene, where the Lady is in her boudoir. I had to wear a terrible dress, in a dull green colour and sleeveless, with a golden belt. My upper arms were never very pretty, and I had to wear long hair. All this together with the bad direction; I felt very unhappy. That first scene gave me a bad start. In later scenes my costumes and the wig they gave me were more appropriate, so I was able to make up a bit of the initial bad impression. After my fiasco with the Lady I was not cast much any more for quite some time. Next I played Laura in Tennessee Williams's *Glasmenagerie*. I was left to work properly, and was good again. The artistic director of course saw me in that and then cast me as Olivia in *Twelfth Night*, where I was good again. Throughout, though, they had the habit of scheduling very long rehearsals, so we had hardly any time to learn our lines, what with performances at the same time, so the prompt would read all the lines all the time. I asked her not to do this for me, but she did it all the same, and it drove me insane, hearing my lines from the side of the stage all the time. It was impossible for me to concentrate from within.

In the Oldenburg production of *My Fair Lady*, I was Mrs Pierce. The girlfriend of the director played Eliza, and thus she had most of the director's attention during rehearsals.

DMD
You mentioned having Inge Langen in mind when you played the Lady in *Kabale und Liebe* in Flensburg. Was that the only such occasion when your own acting was inspired by the performance of another actress:

UD
No. When I played the part of Emily in *Our Town* in Düsseldorf, I always had Elfriede Kuzmany's voice in my ear, her way of playing the role in Bremen some years back when I was Becky. I did not imitate her consciously, but her performance influenced me intuitively. I had seen *Undine* in Düsseldorf, with Käthe Gold[23] as Undine. That was still very vivid in my memory and I played with Gold in my mind, intuitively, in Wilhelmshaven. My first role in Oldenburg was Sidonie Knobbe in *Die Ratten*. I remembered Sybille Binder[24] from Düsseldorf in that part; from the first rehearsal onwards I was ok and the director did not have to work with me much.

I had played Solange in very good productions of Genet's *The Maids* in Cuxhaven and Oldenburg. In Neuss, I played Madam. I did not feel well because of the costume. We all wore black tights with a long black blouse over. Whereas the colleagues who played the maids had quite shapely legs, my thighs were, I thought, too fat. I played very outwardly, for a change, not from within, again helped by what I remembered from the actresses who had played Madam in Cuxhaven and Oldenburg.

DMD
At the beginning of the interview, we talked about your training. Over the years, did directors provide, as part of their rehearsals, further training as such?

UD

In Anouilh's *Orchester* I had lessons in how to hold the violin and how to mime playing it. Apart from that, no.

DMD

Across your career, you played in many productions with colleagues who would later become famous, or who were in the cast because of their current popularity and fame. What was it like to work with them?

UD

In Wunsiedel, Romuald Pekny[25] was Hamlet, already then a star; he was very intensive and precise, very demanding. Horst Mehring was the local star in Oldenburg. He was Professor Higgins in *My Fair Lady* and I played with him in *Danton's Tod*. He commented that I was such a fine team player and was very grateful to me for that. Neuss worked a lot with national stars, well-know from film and television. They served as special devices to attract audiences. They earned a lot, much more than permanent members of the company; they also had their own dressing rooms and got special attention from the dressers. Some demanded special attention from the director, as well, and usually received it. I remember one who had a red carpet put into her dressing room every night. In most cases the stars were very collegial and nice, and very good professionally. They usually did not upstage us intentionally, but I remember one part, later, after my permanent contract in Neuss, where the star actor also directed and I played most of my scenes with the back of my head to the audience, facing the star who was behind me on stage. One production had Ingrid van Bergen as the star—she notoriously killed her lover a few years later and ended in jail. In *Rosmersholm*, the star of the show returned to the stage after having served several years in prison for manslaughter. I tried to be nice to him, but he just literally ignored me, and convinced the young and inexperienced director to change the last scene of the play so as to reduce any impact I could make there as the housekeeper. I took this to the artistic director of the theatre, and he managed to restore at least some of the ending as scripted by Ibsen. During my freelance years, from 1975 until my retirement in 1987, I played alongside stars a number of times. Again, in most cases it was a very rewarding experience. On one tour, one star actress distributed food and cake to the entire cast every night after the performance, back at the hotel. A few weeks into the run the male star actor in the show quietly suggested to me to eat less, because I was getting too fat. Another star actor would stand on stage like a statue, playing staunchly to the audience only, non-existent, as it were, to the other actors on stage with him. It was very difficult to work with him because it was impossible for any atmosphere to develop on stage.

DMD
Talking about atmosphere—could you describe any special experiences you had in the theatre while performing?

UD
I can recall two such experiences. In Solingen, playing Estelle in Sartre's *No Exit*, the atmosphere at the small theatre was always very dense and the audience was very good. I had the feeling that every nerve of my spinal chord was attached to one member of the audience. I never felt that again anywhere else. It was very powerful, coming from the spinal chord.

The second was on tour to South America with Rémond, in Montevideo; the theatre was all wood inside. In the scene between Luise and Lady Milford, Luise's sadness comes out, bursts out. I had the feeling that the entire stage and the entire auditorium were filled with my sadness. Not in relation to the spine, as in Solingen, but from the centre of the chest, my sadness filled the entire space. I was present in the entire room.

Notes

Ursula Dinkgräfe was born Ursula Eleonore Meyer-Dinkgräfe in 1927. She took acting lessons with Herbert Sebald in Bremen from 1945; during her 40-year career as a stage actress, she worked as member of the companies in Bremen, Solingen, Düsseldorfer Schauspielhaus (under the leadership of Gustaf Gründgens), Fritz Rémond Theater in Frankfurt, Heidelberg, Hannover, Kiel, Cuxhaven, Flensburg, Oldenburg and Neuss, and appeared as a guest performer at the theatres in Detmold, Stuttgart (Komödie im Marquardt), Wunsiedel, Ingolstadt, Düsseldorf (Komödie, Kammerspiele), Bad Godesberg (Kleines Theater im Park), Heidelberg (Zimmertheater), Neuwied, and Castrop Rauxel. She appeared in a film with Lilli Palmer (*Eine Frau, die weiß, was sie will*) and in a number of televised stage productions and other programs on television. In 1987 she retired and has lived with her son and his family in Wales since 1994. See http://users.aber.ac.uk/dam/title.html for a documentation of her career with production photos and press cuttings. See also Daniel Meyer-Dinkgräfe (ed). *Ein Kabinettstück der Schauspielkunst / A Showpiece of the Art of Acting: Ursula Dinkgräfes Bühnenlaufbahn / Ursula Dinkgräfe's stage career*. Newcastle: Cambridge Scholars Press, 2007.
1 BDM is the abbreviation for Bund Deutscher Mädels (Federation of German Girls), a Nazi youth organisation.
2 Heinrich Koch (1912-2006), German theatre director and Intendant

3 Herbert Sebald was a German stage actor who worked mainly in Bremen.

4 Gillis van Rappard started his career as an actor, director and Intendant in Bremen. In 1961 he took over the Zimmertheater in Heidelberg, which he led until he retired in 1985 at the age of

5 Elfriede Kuzmany (1915-2006), German stage and screen actress.

6 Wolf Rathjen (1923-2003), German stage and film actor and director, Intendant.

7 Elisabeth Flickenschild (1905-1977), German stage and screen actress)

8 Gustaf Gründgens (1899-1963), German stage and film actor, director and Intendant.

9 Peter Gorski (b. 1921), adopted son of Gustaf Gründgens, director.

10 Jürgen Goslar (b. 1927), German stage and screen actor

11 Hans Müller Westernhagen (1918-1963), German stage actor and director.

12 Maximilian Schell (b. 1930), Swiss-Austrian stage and screen actor and director.

13 Fritz Rémond (1902-1976) was a German actor, director and artistic director, cousin of actor and playwright Curt Goetz. Until 1936, Rémond lived in Prague as an actor; in 1947, he founded the Kleines Theater im Zoo in Frankfurt/Main in a building that originally formed part of the Frankfurt Zoo. The suggestion to start that theatre came from the zoo's director, Bernard Grzimek.

14 Gré Brouwenstijn (1915-1999), Dutch soprano.

15 Wolfgang Windgassen (1914-1974), German Heldentenor.

16 Berthold Sakmann founded the *Komödie im Marquardt* in Stuttgart in 1951 and remained its Intendant until 1985.

17 Wilhelm List-Diehl, German stage actor, director, was Intendant at the Staatstheater Oldenburg from 1965-8, after that until 1980 in Konstanz.

18 Harry Niemann was Intendant at the Staatstheater Oldenburg from 1968 to 1985.

19 Hermann Wetzke was Intendant of the Rheinisches Landestheater in Neuss from 1967 to 1978.

20 Ulrich Erfurth (1910-1986), German actor and director.

21 Yvonne de Carlo (1922-2007), American screen actress.

22 Inge Langen (b. 1924) German stage and screen actress.

23 Käthe Gold (1907-1997), Austrian stage and film actress.

24 Sybille Binder (1892-1962), Austrian stage and film actress.

25 Romuald Pekny (b.1920), Austrian stage and screen actor.

BIBLIOGRAPHY

Ayckbourn, Alan. 1982. *Season's Greetings*. London: Samuel French.

Brahms, Caryl and Ned Sherin. *Beecham*. Playscrips 899.

Clark, Brian. 1978. *Whose Life is it Anyway?* Ashover: Amber Lane.

—. 1986. *The Petition*. Oxford: Amber Lane.

Churchill, Caryl. 1991. *Top Girls*. London: Methuen.

Dietrich, Margaret. 1974. *Das Moderne Drama*. Stuttgart: Kröner.

Drucker, Vanessa. *No Regrets*. Playscript 1413

Enkemann, Jürgen. 1980. Politisches Alternativtheater in Großbritannien. *EASt* 2.

Frayn, Michael. 1982. *Noises Off*. London: Methuen.

Friel, Brian. 1981. *Translations*. London: Faber and Faber.

Gems, Pam. 1979. *Piaf*, Oxford: Amber Lane

Gray, Simon. 2002, *Quartermain's Terms*. London: Faber and Faber.

Haida, P. 1973. *Komödie um 1900. Wandlungen des Gattungsschemas von Hauptmann bis Sternheim*, München: Fink.

Hampton, Christopher. 1983. *Tales From Hollywood*. London: Faber and Faber.

—. 1997. *Total Eclipse*. London: Faber and Faber.

Harwood, Ronald. 1980. *The Dresser*. Oxford: Amber Lane Press.

Hastings, Michael. 1985. *Tom and Viv*. Harmondsworth: Penguin.

Hayman, Ronald. 1979. *British Theatre Since 1955: A Reassessment*. Oxford, Oxford University Press.

Hughes, Dusty. 1986. *Futurists* London: Faber and Faber.

Kempinski, Tom. 1981. *Duet for One, London*. London: French.

Leisentritt, Gudrun. 1979. *Das eindimensionale Theater: Beitrag zur Soziologie des Boulevardtheatres*, München, Minverva.

MacDonald, Stephen. 1983. *Not About Heroes: The Friendship of Siegfried Sassoon and Wilfred Owen*. London: Faber and Faber.

Meyer-Dinkgräfe, Daniel. (ed.) 2002. *Who's Who in Contemporary World Theatre*. London: Routledge.

—. 2005. *German Boulevard Comedy*. London: Cambridge Scholars Press.

—. (ed). 2007. *Ein Kabinettstück der Schauspielkunst / A Showpiece of the Art of Acting: Ursula Dinkgräfes Bühnenlaufbahn / Ursula Dinkgräfe's stage career*. London: Cambridge Scholars Press, 2007.

O'Brien, Edna. 1981. *Virginia*. London: Hogarth.
Pownall, David. 1983. *Master Class*. London: Faber and Faber.
—. 2001. *Black Star*, in *Pownall: Plays 2*. London: Oberon Books.
Russell, Willy. 1986. *Educating Rita, Stags and Hens and Blood Brothers: Two Plays and a Musical,* London: Methuen.
Schmitt, Emmanuel. 1997. *Der Freigeist*. Lengwil: Libelle.
Schoell, Konrad. 1970. *Das französische Drama seit dem zweiten Weltkrieg, Bd. 1: Konventionelle Formen von Sartre bis Sagan.* Göttingen: Vandenhoeck und Ruprecht.
Shaffer, Peter. 1984. *Amadeus*. Burnt Mill: Longman.
Taylor, C. P. 1082. *Good*. London: Methuen.
Taylor, John Russell. 1962. *Anger and After: A Guide to the New British Drama*. London: Methuen.
Tynan, Kenneth. Review of *Look Back in Anger*. Reprinted in *A View of the English Stage 1944-1965*, ed. Kenneth Tynan, 176-9. London: Methuen.
Weckherlin, Thorsten. 2001. *Mit Boulevard gegen Dallas. Das Theater von Peter Zadek als kritisches Vergnügen*. Norderstedt, Books on Demand.
Wells, Win. *Gertrude Stein and a Companion*. Playscript 1621.
Werth, Alexander. 1949. *Musical Uproar in Moscow*. London: Turnstile.
Wolter, Jürgen. 1980. Anger als dramatischer Impuls. Gesellschaftskritik und gesellschaftliche Utopie seit 1945. In *Drama und Theater im England des 20. Jahrhunderts*. Ed. Heinz Kosok. Düsseldorf: Bagel.
Young, Phil. 1983. *Crystal Clear*. Harmondsworth: Penguin.

Websites used for biographical information
(all accessed 21 January 2007)

Claus Helmer,
    http://www.diekomoedie.de/komoedie/ensemble/index.html
Joseph Marcell, http://josephmarcell.com/
Miriam Margolyes, http://www.miriammargolyes.com/biography.php
Roger Owen, http://www.aber.ac.uk/tfts/staff/profiles/roo.html
Gareth Potter,
    http://www.cardiffcasting.co.uk/men/CVs/Gareth_Potter.htm
David Ian Rabey, http://www.aber.ac.uk/tfts/staff/profiles/ddr.html
Roland Rees, http://www.oberonbooks.com
Eric Standidge, http://www.playbyplay.co.uk/aboutus.php
David Thorpe, http://www.blogger.com/profile/10930421

Antoinette Walsh,
     http://www.cssd.ac.uk/staff.php/9/68/antoinette_walsh.html
Timothy West,
     http://www.gavinbarkerassociates.co.uk/html/timothy_west.htm
Tom Wilkinson, http://www.hollywood.com/celebs/fulldetail/id/198204
     http://www.tiscali.co.uk/entertainment/film/biographies/tom_wilkinson
     _biog.html, http://www.imdb.com/name/nm0929489/bio

INDEX